OUR WORLD IN TRANSITION

D1531917

Also by Diarmuid O'Murchú:

————

Poverty, Celibacy, and Obedience

Quantum Theology

Reclaiming Spirituality

Religion in Exile

OUR WORLD IN TRANSITION

Making Sense of a Changing World

DIARMUID O'MURCHÚ, MSC

A Crossroad Book
The Crossroad Publishing Company
New York

First published in Great Britain in 1992 by The Book Guild, Ltd.

First published in the United States of America in 2000 by
The Crossroad Publishing Company
481 Eighth Avenue, New York, NY 10001

Copyright © 1992, 1995 by Diarmuid O'Murchú

All rights reserved. No part of this book may be reproduced, stored in a
retrieval system, or transmitted, in any form or by any means, electronic,
mechanical, photocopying, recording, or otherwise, without the written
permission of The Crossroad Publishing Company.

Printed in the United States of America

Library of Congress Card Number: 00-104321

ISBN 0-8245-1862-4

1   2   3   4   5   6   7   8   9   10   04   03   02   01   00

CONTENTS

DEDICATION

You broke through a veil of confusion and pain;
You glimpsed a horizon you just couldn't name.
And your heart it did yearn for what might have been,
The dream of a new world order.

Your memory is etched in this book that I write,
Your dream underpins all its meaning.
Thanks for the gift of your wisdom and love.
Continue, good friend, with your dreaming!

KEITH GOODMAN
(1968-1990)

INTRODUCTION

If you feel the ground shifting beneath your feet; if you don't know what the hell's going on in today's world; if you think Western governments are out of touch with reality and you feel the Churches are talking a language that nobody understands apart from themselves, then this book is for you!

Take a moment to reflect on this statement:

> 'We are living in the greatest revolution in history, a huge, spontaneous upheaval of the entire human race. Not a revolution planned and carried out by any particular party, race or nation, but a deep elemental boiling over of all the inner contra-dictions that have ever been in people, a revolution of the chaotic forces inside everybody. This is not something we have chosen, nor is it anything we are free to avoid.'

Do these words resonate with your experience? You might be surprised to learn that they were written initially in the 1950s by no less prophetic a genius than the late Cistercian monk, Thomas Merton. He was one of several people who began to feel and perceive new vibrationary forces, pulsating right across our world. It was like the birthpangs of new possibilities, a dream being born!

THE VOLATILE 1960s

In a sense, that dream came to birth in the 1960s, one of the most volatile and creative decades of the twentieth century.

7

Planet Earth awoke from a type of delusory daze. We began to discover (or rediscover) our world. For the first time, we heard of a place called the Third World; we were shocked and horrified at the poverty, hunger and deprivation, and we vowed to give as generously as possible. Marshall McLuhan was at the height of his power, proclaiming the gospel of the global village; thousands of young people purchased rucksacks and roamed to the farthest corners of the Earth.

And the powerless began to realize that they need be powerless no more: in 1960 alone, *seventeen* African nations threw off the shackles of colonialism. Throughout the 1960s, Trade Unions reached a new height of prowess and militancy, while student protests all but wrecked the ruling classes of European and American universities. Religion, too, took a hammering; in a few situations it was fleeced as huge numbers of Jesus freaks and flower people abandoned the staid and austere institutions for the charismatic fellowship of 'community' or the inner ecstasy of Yoga and Eastern meditation.

With hindsight, it seems as if we were trying to throw off the old shackles that repressed our joy and creativity as a human species, and with the outburst of fresh energy, almost anything seemed possible. Progressively, the energy sapped and even evaporated; some people remained vibrant, and this vibrancy still enlivens a whole variety of alternative orientations, such as ecology movements, holistic health, alternative technologies, humanistic psychotherapies, new age religions, etc. But much of this creative energy was redirected into the emerging technology, activating the final step for the Industrial Revolution from the *technological* to the *information* age. For the first time in recorded history, over half the population of the USA was involved in processing information: that threshold was crossed in 1977.

So, what has happened to the dream of the 1960s? I wish to suggest that it has not evaporated, but is still very much alive although not nearly as conspicuous as in the mythic revelry of the 1960s. It is the destiny of every *myth* (a vibrant story loaded with meaning and enthusiasm), to become a *belief* pattern (a set of reform guidelines), and, in time, a *normative context* for a whole new way of life. Meanwhile, the major institutions – whose primary task is to guard the stability and security of the status quo – do all in their power to dampen (and even destroy) the myth, which they perceive to be a threat to their integrity. This is the process of polarisation, to which I'll return in the final section of this book.

The 1960s gave birth to a *new* world view. Even a staunchly conservative institution like the Catholic Church found itself carried along by its momentum, a fact that is clearly demonstrated in a document called *The Constitution of the Church in the Modern World (Gaudium et Spes),* one of the most creative statements to emerge from the Second Vatican Council in the early 1960s. It has taken humanity the past twenty-five years to come to grips with the new vision. After the initial shock – which culturally is measured in decades rather than in single years – we are now better equipped to analyse its meaning and grapple with its profound consequences.

A NEW THRESHOLD

The 1960s marked the end of an era, one in which the colonial consciousness of the Western world had imposed an uniform, mechanical, static value system on all humankind. That closed system had outlived its usefulness; it was no longer appropriate, and millions around the world reacted to its oppressive and stifling influence.

As a species, we have shaken off the old consciousness but have not yet established nor accepted our new-found identity. We have experienced the myth (a type of resurrection reawakening, projecting us into a new way of being) but we haven't come to grips with that experience. Baffled and, perhaps, scared of its demands, some are seeking shelter in the old certainties and securities.

We are, therefore, in an in-between period, a time of *transition.* It is an exciting space, but a very disturbing one. The old securities are gone; the new possibilities are still vague, fudgy and, to say the least, ambiguous. The challenge facing all of us is to name what's going on, connect with its energy, and enhance its positive driving force to carry us into the new future.

In this book, I wish to explore briefly – to the benefit of the average reader – the nature of this transition in some of its more obvious manifestations. I do not set out to prove or disprove anything! As far as possible, I am playing the role of a neutral observer biased towards creativity (a paradox that is justified according to both the Christian belief and Einstein's theory of relativity). I am attempting to read the signs of the times and explore their implications for our world, a world living through the throes of change, moving from the old to the promise and challenge of a new vision.

As we approach the third millenium the transition is likely to become more intense and profound. Standard systems and institutions are likely to become more inept and incapable of grappling with the realities of our world. Increasing numbers of people, disillusioned or disorientated, may become embittered, angry and violent.

It is hoped that this book – in however small a way – will help to inform people what the transition is about and how we might begin to cope with its exigencies. Instead of being confounded by perplexity and responding negatively, those who are informed and enlightened can glimpse the hope and promise of a new future. Not alone will that help us to retain our sanity, but more importantly, it enables us to share the joy and thrill of discovery, along with the profound satisfaction that we are contributing to a new lease of life on Earth.

The future can be bright and prosperous – for those who know what's going on!

PART ONE

WHOLES AND PARTS

In our highly mechanised world, most of us have experienced mechanical breakdown, whether it be of the car, the television, the washing-machine or the hair-dryer. And in a highly technological society, these items may be repaired quite readily, so quickly in fact, that we may not comprehend the internal mechanics of the human brain that empowers the technician to do the repair job.

THE MECHANISTIC MODEL

When the mechanic opens the bonnet of the broken-down car, a 'repair-script' immediately comes into action: 'It could be the battery, the plugs, the pistons, the carburetter, etc.' The mechanic is checking the mechanical parts until (s)he finds the faulty one which is then discarded or replaced, or repaired and refurbished.

The underlying principle is quite simple: *The whole equals the sum of the parts.* If all the parts function properly, then the whole (in this case, the car) operates according to plan. Occasionally, all the parts seem to be in working order, yet still the car gives trouble. This leaves the mechanic baffled, and often the salesman, or some other 'go-between' assumes the unpopular role of waffling his way out of an insoluble problem.

It is easy to identify with the car mechanic's approach, but when we learn that a surgeon operates out of an identical mind-set, alarm signals begin to flash. Yes, it's true, the surgeon's job is to repair or replace the disfunctional parts so that the whole (in this case, the human body) can operate appropriately. Sometimes the medic will resort to drugs; what are drugs? I would suggest that they are nothing more than a lubricant to loosen up disfunctional parts. And when they don't work, we try something else. We insist on playing around with the *parts* that are sick, definitely not the *whole*.

In Western society, the principle that the whole equals the sum of the parts underpins all our formal structures and institutions, and it is the major perceptual assumption underpinning the way we understand life. Everything, from the universe to the planet we inhabit, to continents and nations, to major institutions (industrial, educational and ecclesiastical) to individual people, and right down to the new kitchen toaster, is assumed to be *a whole consisting of parts,* which gives it its unique function and identity.

A NEW PARADIGM

The great contradiction we are trying to live with is this: although the principle of the whole being equal to the sum of the parts underpins our way of *doing* things, our mode of *thinking* has shifted to another level. This shift began in the latter half of the nineteenth century and came into its own in the first half of the twentieth century. It is based on a totally different principle which states: *The whole is greater than the sum of the parts!*

Human beings never set out to create this new principle. Why should they, as the alternative one seemed to satisfy all their immediate needs. What, therefore activated the change? In another book (O'Murchú, 1987), I have attempted an answer to this question; here it is adequate to state that the change is being informed by a shift in the quality of *human and planetary consciousness.*

During the course of the twentieth century, we humans began to think, feel, intuit and perceive at a different (higher) level. We may agree with Teilhard de Chardin that we have been pushed into a new stage of evolutionary development; some people find that suggestion too preposterous to be credible. Whatever the reason, we can no longer doubt the perceptual shift into a new way of viewing our world and everything in it; some scholars refer to this as a *paradigm shift* (eg. Kuhn, 1970).

14

In the first part of this book, I will try to explore the implications of the transition from the old principle (and still the dominant one) of *the whole being equal to the sum of the parts,* to the newly-emerging one of *the whole being greater than the sum of the parts.* What the reader needs to keep in mind is that people – whether they are mechanics, doctors, politicians, industrialists, housewives or whatever – do not think out loud in terms of *wholes* or *parts.* My contention is that ninety per cent of our internal thinking is governed by such principles. And it is out of this deeper level that we – all of us – act and make decisions affecting human and earthly life.

How this internal state can affect external behaviour is astutely stated by the American writer John Shea. Adopting spiritualised language, he writes:

'Every person has a faith, a set of presuppositions, which are tested out in everyday life. If this foundational structure is too constricted or self-centred, a crippling lifestyle develops. Attitudes and behaviour become destructive of both self and community. The depth of sin, therefore, is not in the destructive activity itself, but in the consciousness which encourages and validates that activity.'
(John Shea, 1978, p.181).

What these faulty presuppositions are in terms of *wholes* and *parts* is what I propose to examine in Part One. The various examples that I try to unpack and describe will clarify the nature of this transition, one endowed with a basic simplicity, but initially complex and difficult to understand.

The descriptions I offer tend to be outlined in terms of the 'old' and the 'new'. I do not wish to suggest that one is right and the other wrong. In fact, *both are right* for their respective times and cultures. The main point I wish to make is that, today, we find ourselves somewhere along the spectrum between the opposite positions of 'old' and 'new'.

Most of us *have* shifted from the 'old', in its more rigid and antiquarian sense, and very few of us, if indeed anybody, has reached the 'new', because we are still in the process of discovering what the 'new' is. Consequently, we stand on shifting ground. I suspect we are being shifted along by forces we don't quite understand to places we would rather not go. It is this uncomfortable and exciting sense of being *in transition* that I seek to explore in the chapters that follow.

Bibliography

Kuhn, Thomas (1970), *The Structure of Scientific Revolutions,* University of Chicago Press.
O'Murchú, Diarmuid (1987), *Coping With Change in the Modern World,* Cork: Mercier Press, and Leominster: Fowler Wright.
Shea, John (1978), *Stories of God,* Chicago: The Thomas More Press.

1

From Mechanistic to Wholistic Paradigms

The Western myth is crumbling as a result of its own success. The love affair with the machine and secular potency has brought us to the brink of self-annihilation.

Sam Keen

There is a historical backdrop to every cultural transition, one that is immensely important for the transition being considered in this chapter. We need to begin as early as 500 BC, when Greek ideas began to shape and dominate the then-known world. In this ancient wisdom, the universe was considered to be alive, animated by a world soul, just as the human body was enlivened by a personal soul.

According to the ancient Greeks, the universe consisted of earth, air, fire, water and ether. Anaxagoras (500-428 BC) suggested that all matter, in the heavens and on earth, consisted of an infinite number of particles or atoms; Leucippus and Democritus developed these ideas. All cosmic bodies were considered to be divine, and the universe at large was deemed to be a living, organic entity.

These perceptions had a particular application to Planet Earth. Prior to the sixteenth century, there was no such thing as materialism; all matter was sacred, and both the universe and Earth mirrored something of the power and permanence of God, immanent in the created order, as well as being transcendent to it. This spiritual, organic world view, augmented to some extent by a rural, nature-based lifestyle, prevailed to the dawn of the Industrial Revolution in the seventeenth century.

17

THE BIRTH OF CLASSICAL SCIENCE

Under the influence of Newtonian science, Cartesian philosophy and the rudimentary technology of the Industrial Revolution, this world view changed dramatically. The Earth came to be understood as dead, inert matter, to be manipulated and exploited. And the paradigm or model of the living organism was replaced by that of a *machine.* The machine became the working model not merely for the universe and the earth, but for everything on earth, including human beings themselves.

Under Newtonian science, the soul was removed from all aspects of nature. Interestingly and ironically, God was *not* removed; if anything, (s)he was given a new status. God became the supreme mathematician, the inventor of eternal laws who either once or continuously (it is not clear which) wound up the universal time-clock so that it continued to function blindly and rigidly under a predetermined plan. Even Albert Einstein went along with this deterministic view; hence his oft-quoted statement: 'God does not play dice with the universe.'

Progressively, of course, the eternal mathematician was pushed further away, and in conjunction with Pierre Laplace (1749-1827), an increasing number of scientists dismissed God as an unnecessary hypothesis. This was the beginning of scientific reductionism, for which Laplace himself offers the best available description:

> 'An intelligence knowing at any given instant of time, all forces acting in nature, as well as the momentary positions of all things of which the universe consists, would be able to comprehend the motions of the largest bodies of the world and those of the smallest atoms in one single formula, provided it were sufficiently powerful to subject all data to analysis; to it nothing would be uncertain, both future and past would be present before its eyes.'

(quoted in Davies, 1984, p.38)

In this statement, we have the ingredients making up the

world view where the whole (machine) equals the sum of the parts. Mechanistic science had come of age. In large measure, it had been helped by the Protestant Reformation, which, in its excessive devotion to *sola Scriptura* (the Word of God alone), unintentionally desacralised nature, driving yet another wedge between the sacred and the secular. All that related to God came to be focused on the Scriptures; all else belonged to the ungodly realm of the secular, scientific world. Both science and religion must share the blame for the dichotomy that has so shamefully divided these two sources of profound wisdom.

THE MACHINE AS METAPHOR

The mechanistic paradigm, therefore, is the birthchild of the late Middle Ages and concurs with the rise of Newtonian science and the Industrial Revolution. It considers everything to be a *machine* and it deems mechanical processes to be purposeless, and governed by eternal, divine laws. It does not seek to understand the world; it strives to control, manipulate and engineer the universe. Most deadly of all, it sets humans (especially men) over against the created order. It initiates a battle for supremacy; the world is there to be conquered!

In large measure, this model contributed to the growth and expansion of the Industrial Revolution and its immense benefits for humankind. It has also left our world in something of a technological and ecological mess, and it is the growing awareness of these negative features that has led to a reassessment and a progressive rejection of the mechanistic world view.

In fact, the mechanical model has been crumbling since the mid-nineteenth century when James Maxwell united electricity and magnetism into a single theory of electro-magnetism, thus creating the first unified field. With the development of field theory and the subsequent discovery of the four forces – gravitation, electromagnetism, the weak force and the strong force – physicists recaptured the sense of an *alive* and *inherently creative* universe. The *machine* did not need the external, divine driving force. The mechanical model was becoming progressively cumbersome and did not make sense to the emerging world view.

As we move into the twentieth century, the 'world as a machine' becomes even more irrelevant. Despite his mechanistic orientation, Einstein dealt a deadly blow to the Newtonian paradigm by declaring that the experimenter can influence the experiment – even quite profoundly. Human perceptions can modify – dare we say, determine – reality. Although Einstein could never accept it, the relativity theory paved the way for the Quantum theory, which effectively declared the mechanistic world view to be moribund, and brought into being the alternative wholistic paradigm which we'll presently explore.

REDISCOVERING THE ALIVE UNIVERSE

The Danish physicist Neils Bohr was one of the architects of Quantum theory. So fascinated and enthralled was Bohr with the sheer mystery of the universe that he once declared that Quantum theory to be inexplicable: anyone who claimed to have understood Quantum theory had definitely missed the point.

Essentially, Quantum theory claims that we perceive reality, not in isolated bits and pieces (particles, or parts of the whole), but in 'quanta' or what we might call 'lumps of experience'. Therefore, we can never measure accurately what we are perceiving or exploring – the reality is always greater and more complex (more mysterious?) than what we observe or perceive.

Quantum theory, which I'll describe in Chapter Four, is one of the most fascinating and mystical discoveries of all time. Not alone is it a recapitulation of the pre-Newtonian 'alive' universe, but it is a radically new interpretation of that fact. The Greeks perceived the universe to be alive because it had been enlivened by an indestructible power called 'soul'; the real life, namely God, existed outside the universe. According to Quantum theory, the real life is *within*, not outside.

Prior to the discovery of Quantum theory, scientists were preoccupied with the discovery of the basic building blocks – the parts that comprise the whole. J J Thompson named these building blocks 'atoms' in the late nineteenth century. In our attempts to discover the essential nature of the universe, we split the atom, and continued to split it again and again. Then we started bashing it to pieces in powerful particle-accelerators, of which CERN (European Centre for Nuclear Research), near Geneva, is one of the best known. The 'bashing' eventually led to the discovery of *quarks* in the 1960s and right through to the mid-1980s.

So far, nobody has succeeded in smashing a quark. All attempts to do so have failed, which may well mean that we have discovered the ultimate building blocks, which theoretically should be isolated entities out of which everything else is made. For a start, the scientific discoveries confirm that the quarks are *not* entities; nobody has ever seen one, and scientists agree that they are not objects but rather wave-like patterns of energy. Secondly, we have not succeeded in *isolating* them: they can only be studied and understood in pairs or in triads. All of which seems to suggest that ultimately, our world consists of *relationships of energy*, which is exactly what Quantum theory postulated in the 1920s and 1930s.

THE WHOLISTIC PERSPECTIVE

This long digression into history and science has been necessary to understand what may be the single most important transition taking place in today's world, namely, from a *mechanistic* to a *wholistic* understanding of our world and everything in it. What I mean by those terms I can now explain by drawing on a familiar example from medical practice.

Suppose I get a pain in my abdomen. I go to my doctor, who examines the area of the pain and prescribes drugs. The drugs do not work, so I am sent for an X-ray, which is carried out on the affected area. Eventually, surgery is prescribed and this is performed in the abdominal area. Hopefully that remedies my problem; often it doesn't.

Instead of going to my general practitioner in the first place, let us assume I go to a Chinese doctor who specialises in alternative therapies. The consultation may not begin (most likely, will not) with a thorough examination of the sick part. Instead, there ensues a long conversation, a type of interview.

21

I am questioned about the quality of my lifestyle, my relationships, my work, my diet, the extent to which I exercise and relax, my spiritual life (perhaps) and finally, a physical examination.

In the first case, we have an orthodox medic operating out of a mechanistic mind-set (the prevalent model in contemporary medical school and practice), who considers the body to be a machine made up of parts. A part in my abdomen is malfunctioning; the doctor's brief is to intervene and rectify the faulty part using the techniques at his disposal, normally drugs or surgery.

The Chinese doctor adopts a totally different approach and works on the assumption that the whole of my body (and my life) is greater than the sum of my bodily parts. The sick part is probably a *symptom* of a malfunctioning whole; therefore, (s)he focuses on the *whole* (the overall lifestyle) in an attempt to bring balance and harmony into the overall pattern of energy and relationships that comprise the total self; then the part is capable of healing itself. The wholistic model assumes that my body has the innate ability to heal all its ills, provided I allow it to do so (cf. Harrison, 1984).

Wholism is not just about thinking big or globally, which can often be an escape into childish generalities. It is much more than that. It is an invitation to let go of our chauvinistic and manipulative urge to dominate and control everything in our universe. At a deeper level, it is a call to acknowledge and appreciate that everything (including humans) belongs to a greater whole; that all life forms are interdependent and need each other; that everything thrives, not in isolation and competition, but in mutual cooperation.

The wholistic paradigm seeks to draw attention to the creative complexity of life. It reminds us that our world is animated by an evolutionary design in which all the parts serve the greater whole and only find their true meaning in cooperating with the whole. If the whole is allowed to function appropriately, then the parts thrive. But if we keep addressing the parts while ignoring (or damaging) the whole, then things can get dangerously out of hand, as is happening extensively in today's world.

Politically and economically, our world has not acknowledged this new way of addressing reality. Nations act in relative isolation, often in jealous and destructive competition. Western powers grossly exploit the natural resources in many parts of the Southern hemisphere, as if North and South were independent entities. We pollute seas and contaminate land for selfish gain and profit. Meanwhile, the planet heads for ecological catastrophe because we have lost our sense of balance and our feel for the whole of life.

It is this urgent and serious global threat that gives credibility to the wholistic paradigm. Without appropriate global strategies and policies – at the global (wholistic) level – there may be no planet to inhabit as we move into the twenty-first century. In fact, it now looks as if it will take a catastrophe of global magnitude to thrust us into this new consciousness and create something akin to a world government – an inspiration initially articulated in the birth of the United Nations, some fifty years ago.

At an universal level, the wholistic paradigm makes a great deal of sense. Indeed, it seems the only sane and rational way forward for our threatened planet, although few governments acknowledge this fact. Increasingly, people are also identifying the personal significance of the wholistic vision. Medically, we realize that healing has as much to do with a clean environment, a balanced lifestyle and a peaceful mind, as it has with a healthily functioning body. Educationally, we sense that a points system geared to good examination results is severely limiting and may, in fact, inhibit growth and creativity. Spiritually, we are beginning to appreciate that faith means much more than allegiance to one or other belief system.

The most compelling proof that we are moving from mechanistic to wholistic approaches is the breakdown of so many mechanistic models. Mechanisation has brought many benefits to humankind, especially in Western, industrialised nations, but because mechanisation has become a God of power and profit, its destructive side-effects are outpacing its positive achievements. The more powerful Western technology becomes, the more we will continue to exploit natural resources, especially in the Southern hemisphere. The more we allow the machine to become a power-symbol, the more we'll create weaponry of war that becomes outlandishly lethal.

So much of what goes on in our world today makes nonsense while we continue to think and act in terms of nation competing with nation, and continent with continent. The major issues confronting our world, ones that now touch the lives of billions all over the earth, can only be addressed appropriately through a global strategy, under a world view that is essentially *wholistic*.

The example from contemporary medical practice illustrates how the transition is beginning to affect our individual and personal lives. Throughout the twentieth century, medicine has had many breakthroughs. Yet sickness is rampant, new diseases surface annually and every nation on earth spends millions on healthcare. Despite all the breakthroughs, we have not learned to live as healthier people. Why? Because essentially we are not taught or encouraged to be responsible for our health. Instead we have been brainwashed into a childish dependency on a 'health-mechanic', called a doctor. As 'whole' people, we have a higher destiny than this. The time has come to take responsibility for what we are essentially meant to be.

The mechanistic model served us well throughout the Industrial era. Now that we have moved into an Information age, we need a new model, one that will allow us to stretch our intelligence, vision and imagination, one that will enable us to live creatively and responsibly in a world made small and intimate by travel, communication and computerisation. The fuller implications of the transition to the wholistic future become clearer as we explore the transitions outlined in subsequent chapters. Meanwhile, the considerations of this Chapter are drawn together in the resume chart below.

MAIN FEATURES OF TWO PARADIGMS

MECHANISTIC	WHOLISTIC
1. The whole equals the sum of the parts	The whole is greater than the sum of the parts
2. Every system or structure consists of isolated, unrelated, autonomous parts	Everything consists of parts continually interrelating, a process characterised by interdependence and mutual cooperation.
3. Basic metaphor is the machine	Basic metaphor is the *holon* (the whole).
4. Change or repair demands mechanical interference and manipulation	All life-forms have an innate self-organising potential which is undermined by mechanical interference.
5. Every aspect is studied through observation, quantification, dissection and manipulation.	Since the whole is greater than the sum of the parts, our understanding is always partial and must remain open to new and fuller understanding.
6. Modification and change is effected from outside.	Change and healing is effected from within, possibly by a change-agent acting from without.
7. We can control the machine, and therefore we model everything on mechanical processes.	We don't need to control – trust the unfolding process.

8. Objectivity and emotional non-involvement are the basic virtues.	Participation and a feeling for the whole are the basic virtues.

Bibliography:

Capra, Fritjof (1984), *The Turning Point,* Flamingo Books.

Davies, Paul C W (1984), *Superforce,* Heinemann.
    (1988), *The Cosmic Blueprint,* Heinemann.

Harrison, John (1984). *Love Your Disease,* London: Angus and Robertson.

2

From a Static to a Dynamic World View

*We are getting used to the idea that adulthood is not static.
We are coming to terms with the insight that change is
normative, continuous and consequential.*

James W Fowler

To survive meaningfully on Earth, we humans need a measure
of stability and predictability. We feel more comfortable when
things happen on a regular, structured basis. We also like
variety and novelty; we unconsciously welcome these within
the boundaries of what is already known and familiar.

At a global level, too, we desire structure and stability. We
have inherited a long tradition of a universe, created by God,
which was deemed to be perfect and unchanging. Plato
observed that, although we are aware of change on a local and
daily basis, over the aeons nothing really changes; essentially,
our world remains static and stable.

HISTORICAL BACKGROUND

Newtonian science strongly endorsed the concept of a static
universe in which all change could be explained in terms of
local modifications within the great, eternal, unchanging
machine. Even Einstein endorsed this view, favouring it to the
contemporary conviction that the universe was either
contracting or expanding (Hubble's discovery of the 1920s).
To wield his way out of this dilemma, Einstein added a fudge
factor known as the cosmological constant.

Once again, it was in the nineteenth century that we
perceived the limitations of the static world view. The simple

27

hierarchy, beginning with God at the top and descending through angels, human beings, animals to ever lower forms of life, was the accepted model. The number of species was fixed; it had not changed since the beginning of creation.

One of the first people to challenge these views was Jean Baptiste Lamarck (1744-1829), who suggested that all beings evolved from earlier, simpler forms under the pressure of their environment. Several decades later, Charles Darwin (1809-1882) presented an overwhelming mass of evidence in favour of biological evolution. The previous conception of the world as a machine fully constructed from the hands of the creator progressively gave pride of place to an evolving and ever-changing universal system, in which complex structures developed from simpler forms.

Darwin's influence prevailed – although somewhat subdued – until the 1960s, when the Big Bang theory became widely accepted as an explanation for the origin of the universe. The Big Bang does not speculate on the origins of life at large; it explains how the universe commenced as a gaseous explosion, progressively settling down into the various forms and patterns of life we now know, but also (and this is the important bit) initiating the process of an expanding universe, which has been 'stretching' and evolving ever since.

THE PERSISTENCE OF CHANGE

The fact that we live in a world that is continually changing, evolving and developing is quite strange, and even alien, to most people. The fact that our human bodies and personalities change and grow is something we are not well attuned to. Most people perceive change to be disruptive, threatening our peace and stability, endangering our future. Although we don't always deliberately and explicitly create a stable, static environment, it is one of our strongest and most pervasive desires.

The transition, therefore, from a static to a dynamic (changing) world view is quite complex. For a start, it is not merely a phenomenon of our time. Humanly, ecologically and globally, our world (and we ourselves) has *always* been changing and, no doubt, will continue to do so. Change is of the essence of life. Without this change, new growth would not take place; life would atrophy; stagnation and extinction would ensue.

Therefore, the first challenge facing us today is to realize that change is more natural, desirable, appropriate and essential than non-change if we humans and our world are to realize our God-given potential. But in a world where we have been brainwashed and conditioned into the opposite conviction for so long, it is difficult – impossible for many people – to adjust to this new awareness.

There is no going back to the good old days when things were static and stable, and we all knew 'where we stood'. Even if we could revert, it would be totally inappropriate because our innate destiny is to progress (not regress), to change and adapt to the new challenges of an ever-changing personality and an ever-changing society.

THE INFORMATION AGE

The contemporary transition, therefore, before ever being a critical issue of our time, is a fundamental human, earthly and universal phenomenon. Why, therefore, has it become so acute at the present time? One explanation may be the growth of information technology in the recent past. From the beginning of the Christian era up to the dawn of the scientific revolution (c.1600 AD), our 'quantity' of knowledge doubled that of the three-to-five previous thousand years; between 1600 and 1900 it doubled again, this time taking only three hundred years; it took only *fifty* years for another quantitative leap (up to 1950), followed by yet another shorter time-span of *twenty* years, up to 1970; then *ten* years up to 1980; currently the quantity of information is replicating every three years.

I am not referring to some academic, intellectual exercise taking place at universities or other centres of learning. I am referring to a global trend; we are *all* causing it, and our lives are being transformed by it.

Alongside the expansion of knowledge we note a parallel effort to store relevant information. To scan just the past few hundred years, we have witnessed a progression from museums to laboratories, where data was stored in material and physical form, to libraries where information could be stacked in smaller space because it was now in written form. We then invented microfilms to contain masses of information while simultaneously finding new ways of communicating it, by means of television and subsequently, the video boom. Then came computerisation, culminating in the microchip which in itself can contain a whole library of information.

Here are two parallel developments unprecedented in human history. Knowledge and information seem to be reaching saturation point. Yet corresponding to each new level of attainment is a corresponding 'technology' by which we can contain and control information. The human mind seems to have an inexhaustible reservoir of resourcefulness. The fact that we can utilise our resources as we have been doing in the course of the twentieth century is an abiding verification of Darwin's claim that we selectively exploit our environment for the benefit of our survival and progress. In other words, precisely because we can and do *change* so dramatically, we succeed in keeping pace with the evolution of universal life.

My contention, however, is that this change and adaptation takes place largely without our being aware of it. We are swept along in a flurry of change, over which we feel we have no control and which we resist rather than enhance in the face of uncertainty. When we do resist, we tend to re-entrench, and hanker for the comfort and security of the illusive stability.

CHIEF CHARACTERISTICS OF TWO WORLD VIEWS

STATIC	DYNAMIC
1. Nothing ever really changes – all change is superficial.	Change is real – growth and progress depend on it.
2. Stability is the basic virtue; 'Don't rock the boat'.	Movement is the nature of life; 'If the boat sinks, we can swim'.

3. Progress is cyclic – essentially the same process repeated over and over.	Progress is evolutionary, cyclic in nature, but each cycle is qualitatively different from every other.
4. Everything in life is complete in itself, self-contained and self-explanatory.	All life-forms, including 'inert' matter, exist and grow in mutual inter-dependence.
5. Individualism and isolation are key qualities.	Nothing can be fully understood in isolation. The individual discovers his true identity in 'community'.
6. If things remain the same, we know where we stand with reality. Too much change disorientates people.	Too much of the same stultifies growth, suffocating creativity and imagination.
7. This is the way God made things; creation is complete.	God continually co-creates, in conjunction with human beings.

COPING WITH CHANGE

Thus far we have survived in our ambivalent ignorance of change, but the future may be a great deal more precarious, and the adjustment to the rapidly changing situation may not continue to happen as spontaneously as in the past. The accelerated pace in the accumulation of knowledge and information is merely one symptom of a universe in change. Such dramatic changes, instigated probably by a new thrust in our evolution as a human species (see Chapter Twelve), are taking place in all spheres of contemporary life. By the end of the present millenium, we'll be much more consciously aware of their impact on every aspect of our daily lives.

The first challenge posed by the static-dynamic transition is one of becoming *aware* of what's going on in our world. The old, static structure is crumbling – in science, religion, politics, economics etc. New dynamic possibilities – highly fluid and flexible – are being explored. Although not yet established in any type of identifiable form, some are profoundly affecting our lives, eg. the information explosion.

A second challenge is to develop *skills* to adjust to this changing environment. We need ways and means of obtaining relevant information. We need associates with whom we can discuss, explore and discern what's going on. And we need meaningful networks of like-minded people, so that together we can keep abreast of a movement that we can't hope to cope with on our own.

In a word, we need to learn how to flow with the momentum of change. *Resisting* is pointless – we only lose out. *Tolerating* it is a meaningless, apathetic response. Learning to flow with it is the only way we can utilise it to our own benefit and to the advantage of universal life. And, enlightened by our wholistic consciousness, let us remember, we have, within us and among us, all the resources we need, not merely to cope, but to advance towards the emerging new world that is on its way.

Bibliography:

Lindfield, Michael (1986), *The Dance of Change: An Eco-spiritual Approach To Transformation,* London & New York: Arkana.

O'Murchú, Diarmuid, (1987), *Coping with Change in the Modern World,* Cork: Mercier Press & Leominster: Fowler Wright.

Russell, Peter (1982), *The Awakening Earth,* Routledge & Kegan Paul.

3

From Closed to Open Systems

Our task must be to free ourselves from this prison by widening our circle of compassion, to embrace all living creatures and the whole of nature in its beauty.
Albert Einstein

In our Western world, private ownership is considered to be a basic human right. We understand this to mean that individuals and families are entitled to possess and own their own home and whatever belongings are deemed desirable for a meaningful and useful life. It is assumed, therefore, that most people own a house, a car, household goods and a certain amount of wealth over which they have exclusive rights for use and ownership.

Some religions, such as Christianity and Islam, encourage and validate private property over and above communal ownership. The religions argue that the former is a prerequisite for the dignity and worth of the individual person and for the uniqueness of the family, perceived by many religions to be the central institution of human civilisation.

The concept of private ownership is something of a misnomer. Many people in underdeveloped nations have more real claim to their small patch of land than wealthy businessmen in Europe or in the USA, who often accumulate much money, but spend it paying off excessive taxes and exorbitant mortgages on properties they do not really own. The religious claim that private property safeguards the uniqueness and dignity of the person and family is a questionable value in a society growing daily more aware of the need for mutual interdependence. Other considerations apart, the notion is a relatively recent one (nineteenth and twentieth centuries) in human civilisation.

In fact, private ownership is largely a byproduct of the mechanistic consciousness referred to in previous chapters. It is the result of breaking the *whole* into subsistent and independent *parts* each presumed to be self-contained and self-sufficient in its own right. One could push this argument farther back and claim that private property is the final outcome of the fragmentation of the land, which commenced about 8000 BC at the dawn of the Agricultural Revolution.

Prior to that time, nations did not even exist. Humans roamed the earth, knowing no national or racial barriers. Some will argue that the creation of private property is the final outcome of a process of cultural refinement; others (like Karl Marx's followers) will profoundly disagree with that interpretation, mustering a great deal of evidence to indicate that our pursuit of privacy is a veneer for extensive and lethal exploitation of people and land alike.

CLOSED AND ISOLATED

The concept of private ownership serves as a good example of the transition from closed to open systems, being explored in this chapter. Closed systems are presumed to be self-contained, self-sufficient, needing nothing or nobody from outside their clearly-defined parameters. The situation is rarely as perfect as that, but comes quite close to it, as we can glean from many of the original manufacturing units in Britain of the seventeenth and eighteenth centuries. In the woollen industry, for example, the raw material was obtained from local sheep farms, often on a fixed contract, over a long number of years. The factory had its own staff for all the various functions ranging from technicians to office personnel, sales people, caterers etc. And the market – aimed largely if not exclusively at the local catchment area – operated from within, or close to, the factory itself.

Today, it is a vastly different scene. The small electronics factory in London may be owned by a group of entrepreneurs living in other continents. The raw material is most likely imported, and may have been procured in a grossly immoral and exploitative manner. Technical, commercial, catering and even managerial staff may be employed from a variety of 'service' agencies. And the market may be as much an overseas as a local one.

What has happened in the industrial sphere is only one symptom of a transition that continues to take place right across our world from closed, local, self-referent projects to ones that are open, non-local and dependent on a vast range of other agencies. In fact, many of the 'closed' factories *have* closed – quite literally. And any modern project attempting to operate on a closed-value system will meet a similar demise. The age of closed systems belongs to the past.

At a broader level, we detect a similar orientation in the religious sphere. Up to about 1960, the Catholic Church staunchly and unashamedly declared: 'Outside the Church there's no salvation'. In the eyes of Catholicism (and to be fair, all the Christian churches adopted this outlook, but not as blatantly as Catholicism), all other believers – and non-believers – were pagans, condemned and damned for all eternity. Ironically, Catholicism rarely stated its conviction as crudely as that, which is a subtle and devious feature of all closed systems: the adherents themselves tend to be locked into a blind ideology which, deep in their hearts, they know to be false, or at least inappropriate.

In fact, prior to 1960, most major social, political and ecclesiastical institutions operated the closed-system model. Despite the launching of the United Nations in 1945, the development of NATO in 1949, or even the Warsaw Pact in 1955, most nations continued to function in relative and competitive isolation. Even international trade and commerce was perceived as an acquisition of foreign goods for *our* economy. There was no sense of international interdependence. Consequently, the resources of weaker nations were savagely and ruthlessly exploited. Even now, Western nations continue to do the same thing, something that was at least forgivable amid the ignorance of bygone days, but totally unpardonable in an ecologically threatened planet.

Within nations, various institutions and services worked autonomously, often duplicating what was being offered and unconsciously squandering valuable resources. In most

European governments, inter-departmental cooperation is largely unknown. Health, education, social services, civil law tend to work in isolation, an anomaly that often comes to light in a probationer's office as the different 'services' encounter one another in trying to resolve a personal or social deviancy; one wonders at times where the greater deviancy rests; within the 'offender' or within the 'services' trying to help the offender. Coordination of services, still in its early stages, tends to be instigated by some creative (perhaps confused) networker, often operating on the fringe of, if not outside, the mainstream system.

FUTURE OF THE FAMILY

Nowhere is the closed system disintegrating so persuasively as in family life. This is an interesting and fascinating paradox. Traditionally, the family is considered to be the central and most stable unit of society. Long before religions sanctioned the family as God's own creation, people safeguarded marriage, the home and the family unit as cherished objectives of a mature and developed culture. Many prehistoric cultures had elaborate rituals and prescriptive regulations governing marital status and sexual behaviour.

Since 1960 a great deal has changed, especially in the Western world. Sexuality is no longer concomitant with procreation. In the contemporary world, sexuality is seen more as an articulation and expression of human intimacy. Neither is sexuality limited to marriage: extra-marital relations – temporary or permanent – have become common. Even homosexual or lesbian partnerships have attained a certain degree of acceptability.

As for marriage itself, the lifelong bond – even when sanctioned by Church law – is more an exception than a norm. Many people may have up to three different partners in a single lifetime. And home life is changing from being a relatively stable, regularly-patterned base, to becoming something more akin to a boarding house for bed, breakfast and evening meal.

In noting these changes, I am neither condemning nor condoning. I am trying to observe – openly and honestly –

contemporary trends which so many people choose to ignore, matters on which legislators allow themselves to be wooed by the most persuasive lobbiers of one or other extreme position, while churches continue to preach outdated moralities. So few people are attempting an in-depth analysis of what's going on around us, touching the very fabric of our daily lives, throwing our value system into chaos and confusion (in some cases, leaving us with no value system at all), and projecting future generations into a world so open-ended as to be psychologically and spiritually devastating.

The nuclear family – consisting of father, mother, 2.2 children, the dog, two cars, their own house etc. – is still a common feature in the Western world, especially among the so-called upper and middle classes. But it is a system corroding at the base, collapsing under the impact of some nebulous, internal malaise. Perhaps Ronald Laing, the one time radical British psychiatrist, was correct in suggesting, some twenty years ago, that the family was the breeding ground for neurosis and psychosis. It is still a valid way of living, but has become so closed-in on itself that it would seem to be collapsing under the strain of internal pressure.

I am not suggesting that other forms of marital and family lifestyle (as referred to above) are appropriate alternatives; we can be fairly sure they are not. Instead, they may be viewed as the *symptoms* of a changing consciousness, from closed, self-contained systems to more open, fluid and flexible possibilities. We may not like the new developments – and many concerned people of Church and State alike will continue to condemn them – but if we don't strive to understand something of the *underlying* meaning, then we cannot contribute constructively to the emerging alternatives.

For many people, the transition from closed to open systems is a difficult one to grasp. We have been so conditioned – through formation, education, training etc. – to think and act in closed-system terms, that we have been largely oblivious to what has been happening around us in the past twenty years. The transition I refer to is not something that we expect to happen at some point in the future. It *has* been happening with such momentum over the past few decades that it is now irreversible. Ignoring it, or fighting against it, will get us nowhere!

The only appropriate and trustworthy response is to acknowledge it for what it is – not a set of superficial, chance happenings, instigated by irresponsible freaks, but a profound change in human consciousness, activated (most likely) by evolutionary forces of global magnitude; the challenge facing us is to channel its energy into more creative and constructive avenues. This may demand wholly new ways of acting, behaving and living together on Planet Earth.

ORDER OUT OF CHAOS

My final example of the shift from closed to open systems may be considered to be the most provocative of all. Again, it is largely unacknowledged, although scientifically established since 1977, when the Belgian biochemist, Ilya Prigogine, obtained the Nobel Prize for his theory of dissipative structures.

Prigogine's work is based on a daring and adventurous vision. He set out to challenge the Second Law of Thermodynamics, which was at that time, and still is, an unquestioned dogma of mainstream science. According to the Second Law, everything in our universe moves in the direction of greater disorder, waste and inefficiency, towards what the scientists call *entropy* (the measure of the unavailability of energy for re-use). A piece of coal is thrown into the fire; it can never be used again. An inkblot cannot be returned to its original usable state of a concentrated drop. In this view, the universe is progressively wearing itself out and, will eventually grind to a halt.

Advocates of the Second Law point to such trends as rising social unrest, increased crime, growing economic chaos, as cultural indicators of the world system in decline; they consider deforestation, environmental pollution and the exploitation of natural and mineral resources as symptoms of the 'disease' that will culminate in the heat-death.

At face value, the trend would certainly seem to be irreversible, moving towards greater and greater destruction. On the part of Prigogine, it took something of a mystic's vision and a martyr's courage to challenge this view. To obtain a

Nobel Prize for his effort must be one of the scientific miracles of the twentieth century.

Mathematically, Prigogine's experiments are complicated and elaborate, and need not concern us here. A few simple theoretical considerations underpin his vision. Firstly, the Second Law only applies to *closed* systems, not to *open* ones. (Remember, in the Newtonian world view, every system is considered to be a *machine,* consisting of a determined number of parts, and therefore a *closed* entity). According to Prigogine, all living systems are *open*, and inherently interact with the wider environment in the dual role of expelling entropy and taking in energy and matter to replenish depleted resources. Even in a chaotic state, living systems display amazing powers of self-organisation. Unpredictably and often creatively, the system 'leaps' from the lower chaotic levels pointing to breakdown, to higher, more subtle levels, making breakthrough possible.

At a personal level, we now know that parts of the human brain which remain intact after an accident can assist the healing process in damaged parts. The *damage* tends to be clear, measurable and observable; the *healing* is usually unpredictable and often defies scientific (medical) explanation.

At a global level – because our planet is an *open* system – depleting resources may be replenished, or compensated for, by energies from the wider atmosphere. A simple example is that of energy resources: naturally produced ones may well be exhausted by the end of the twenty-first century, but the potential of solar energy is little understood and scarcely explored as yet. I am not suggesting that we should thoughtlessly exploit the former on the assurance that the latter automatically fills the gap; open systems also remind us that our simple, destructive logic is not merely outdated, but could be quite deleterious to future planetary wellbeing.

Prigogine's theory of dissipative structures has many affinities with David Bohm's concept of the implicate and explicate order of universal life. According to Bohm our experience of universal life is twofold: there is the world we observe and experience in daily life, often fragmented, disorientated and disorganised. However, there is also the unmanifest world, the patterns and cycles of nature and the

39

less obvious processes of order (rather than organisation) that underpin and animate our world.

We are told that ever since the Big Bang our universe has been expanding and, apparently, will continue to do so for billions of years yet to come. Among cosmologists, it is widely assumed (and 'proof' is more that of mystical vision than scientific verification) that this expansion, with the hundreds of new planets that 'appear' each year, is a manifestation of a universe growing in harmony, beauty and variety. Contrary to the Second Law, it is not a contracting universe heading towards the doom and destruction of a heat-death.

FEATURES OF THE OPEN SYSTEM

According to Prigogine and his colleagues, open systems are characterised by:

a) **Openness:** Matter and energy are able to flow between the system and its environment; theoretically, this can happen at the level of all living systems, whether that of the human body, a social aggregate, a factory, a nation or the universe itself.

b) **Far from Equilibrium:** When a living system is in perfect equilibrium it is stagnating, closed to new life and therefore heading for extinction. To be open to change, reform, renewal, there has to be a level of inner turmoil, a readiness to let go and part with old ways, a willingness to assume and assimilate new ideas, fresh behaviours – a whole new way of doing things. An open, living system will be characterised by a degree of restlessness, movement, change and growth.

c) **Self-reinforcement:** In scientific language, certain elements of the system catalyse the production of new elements of the same kind. Living systems, in an evolutionary world, are innately creative; it is in their nature to change, evolve and loosen up (catalyse) that which threatens to stifle or arrest growth. When the system is unable to do this *constructively*, inevitably it begins to do it *destructively*, thus eventually paving the way for new possibilities. In our mechanical consciousness, we tend to look for external scapegoats to blame for the damage caused; in the wholistic consciousness, inner and outer forces are perceived to cooperate for the future destiny of all living systems.

When dealing with open systems, we need a whole new attitude of mind and heart. An open system has a type of life of its own, deserving of our respect and gentleness. We have been so conditioned into practices of interference, manipulation, control and exploitation that it is extremely difficult to adopt a stance of allowing and enabling the system to display its own inherent creativity. Instead of opening up to the grandeur and beauty of universal life, we humans have so mechanised the living world that we have created a type of global imprisonment. So many aspects of life are imprisoned and congealed in man-made bureaucracies that our planet is in real danger of perishing from the congestion of life-energies and the repression of life-vision.

The transition from closed to open systems is one of the most delicate and critical issues of our time. Since institutions tend to be self-perpetuating (a tendency of closed systems), all our major institutions, including governments, churches, economic and political systems, are preoccupied with their own survival. Parliamentary procedure, electioneering and voting systems in most Western nations are not for the good of people, nor for the benefit of Planet Earth; their primary purpose (and sometimes their sole one) is the perpetuation of a closed system. Little wonder that increasing numbers of people are disillusioned with the officialdom of both Church and State.

MAIN DIFFERENCES BETWEEN TWO SYSTEMS

CLOSED	OPEN
1. Self-contained and self-explanatory.	Nothing is complete in itself.
2. Tends to surround itself with defensive structures and top-down leaderships.	Tends to explore a variety of structures and leaderships as circumstances demand.

3. Tends to look to the past and cherishes tradition.	Future-oriented; views past-present-future as a continuum.
4. Jealously guards its own space.	Seeks new ways to interact with others.
5. Considers everything outside itself to be alien or, at best, inferior. Tends to suppress those who disagree.	Welcomes opportunities for dialogue with the wider world, which it assumes to be benevolent and potentially enriching.
6. Feels threatened by novel ideas.	Welcomes other views and opinions.
7. Thrives on self-perpetuating myths such as (8) below.	Looks to other agencies for complementary enlightenment and nurturing support.
8. 'Outside the Church there's no salvation.'	'The Church is the believing community which celebrates God's gift of salvation to all people.'

Can we humans muster the good will to effect this transition? Not without a major 'catalyser', in my opinion. What this catalyser (loosener-up) may be, I have no idea. It could be the environmental crisis ecologists forecast; a nuclear fallout perhaps; maybe the depletion of the ozone layer to the point where human life comes under serious threat.

One would like to be more positive, but the reality is that we only wake up to our inhumanity when confronted with grave danger. There is something profoundly illuminating in the Christian conviction that Resurrection (a new way of being) is always preceded by a Calvary (the calamitous dissolution of the old order), a conviction variously expressed by all the major religions of humankind.

It is inconceivable to me that the world's major powers of

either Church or State are going to give up their power or status; that those who exploit our earth for monetary gain are going to change their ways; that the chauvinistic urge to mechanise and control is going to diminish in any way. If we are unwilling to let go of the old for the new order to come into being, then it is we, *humans* rather than the 'future' that will perish.

No force on earth can arrest the forward movement of the evolutionary process. We humans may be the highest life-form on Planet Earth, but we do not own the planet; we do not have ultimate control over it; we cannot, despite all our mechanistic interference, predict (never mind, control) its future unfolding. The planet itself is an open, creative system. The supreme challenge facing us at this time of transition is to acknowledge this fact, respect it for what it is, and act accordingly.

Bibliography:

Bloom, Alan (1987), *The Closing of the American Mind,* Penguin Books.

Prigogine, Ilya (1971), *From Being to Becoming,* San Francisco: Freeman.

Rokeach, Milton (1960), *The Open and Closed Mind,* New York: Basic Books Inc.

4

From Classical to Quantum Science

I have to speak on behalf of the broad global fraternity of practitioners of mechanics. We collectively wish to apologise for having misled the general educated public by spreading ideas about the determinism of systems satisfying Newton's laws of motion which after 1960 were to be proved incorrect.

Sir James Lighthill (Provost of University College London, 1986)

Because of our inherited mechanistic consciousness, we tend to fragment and categorise our life-experience. Everything fits into a slot, and every experience is labelled, for will or for woe. Science is something you do at school or at college; alternatively, it is that esoteric body of knowledge on the basis of which people build bombs or write books about black holes.

Science is presumed to be the invention of the sixteenth century and more specifically of the technological revolution of the twentieth century. But for time immemorial, people have been asking scientific questions and experimenting with scientific solutions. Magic and witchcraft are prehistoric equivalents of contemporary science. The Ancient Greeks speculated that the world consisted of air, water, earth, fire and ether; they also laid the foundations for geometry, a form of mathematics still in use. For a great deal of our human history, science, religion and philosophy were one, a wholistic perception whose inherent wisdom we seem to be rediscovering at the present time.

Our daily lives are embedded in science. Every time I switch on a light-bulb, use a camera, take an aspirin, run a water tap, drive a car or play a computer game, I am being scientific in the full sense of the word. Science is what makes our world go round. All the technology which we use – day in, day out – for a vast variety of purposes, is what science is about. At one level, there is nothing mysterious in it; at another, it is mystery all over!

THE CLASSICAL MODEL

That type of science with which we are quite familiar in daily life, is what we call the *classical* model. It is characterised by:

a) **Cause and effect:** I push the switch and the light comes on. Everything happens as a result of something that causes it to happen.
b) **Determinism:** Retaining the example of the light-bulb, it is predictable that the light comes on when I push the switch – assuming, of course, that the bulb and switch are in working order. Everything in the universe is assumed to work in this predetermined, predictable fashion.
c) **Wholes comprising a certain number of parts:** The light-switch is a whole (machine) in its own right, consisting of a specific number of parts. If the switch does not work, it has to be the result of faulty or damaged parts. Repair or replace the parts and all will be well. Everything in the universe works in similar fashion – we are often told!

The classical world view was – and continues to be – neat, efficient and so easy to comprehend. We knew where we stood with it – at least, we thought we did until the nineteenth century, when it began to dawn on the scientific community that instead of explaining the world, we had in fact, been explaining it away. Face-value impressions were considered to be objective and reliable; what the neutral observer detected and verified in experiment was considered to be reality as reality was.

Atoms, as the basic units comprising all life in the universe, were first named by the Greek philosopher, Anaxagoras (500-428 BC). Atoms were considered to be indivisible and

45

indestructible (hence the term elementary particles), a view that prevailed until the nineteenth century, when physicists such as John Dalton, J J Thompson and Ernest Rutherford began to analyse the composition and nature of the atom. This led (at the beginning of the present century) to the splitting of the atom and a proliferation of subatomic particles, now numbering over one hundred.

Among the most recent subatomic particles are the leptons and quarks. We may be at the end of the line in our pursuit of elementary particles because, so far, the quarks have defied all attempts to split into smaller particles. Most scientists feel that this failure is due to particle accelerators not being big or powerful enough to create the experimental conditions to split (or bash) the quarks; bigger and enormously expensive accelerators are being built in both Europe and the USA.

But not everybody in the scientific community is convinced that bigger, more powerful accelerators are the answer. Indeed, such a response may be quite inappropriate. The world of subatomic particles is not one of dead, inert matter; it is an universe alive with an amazing network of energies, serving four fundamental forces (gravitation, electromagnetism, the weak and strong forces), which scientists are now convinced can be understood as one, all-encompassing creative energy – hence the search for a Grand Unification Theory (GUT) and a Theory of Everything (TOE).

Before reaching the present proliferation of subatomic particles, scientists at the beginning of the present century began to grapple with the elusive and mysterious nature of the subatomic world. Pioneering this search were people like Max Planck from Germany, Niels Bohr from Denmark, Louis de Broglie from France, Erwin Schrodinger and Wolfgang Pauli from Austria, Werner Heisenberg from Germany and Paul Dirac from England.

A new scientific world began to unfold when Max Planck discovered that the energy of heat radiation is not emitted continuously, but appears in the form of energy packets. Einstein called these energy packets *quanta*, and recognised them as functional aspects of nature. The fascinating thing about these quanta is that one could never say for definite whether they were *waves* or *particles* of energy, or whether they could be said to exist at definite places or whether they tended

46

to exist as 'probability waves'. This is the kernel of the *quantum theory,* to which we will return presently.

Already, therefore, in the 1920s, the concept of the world made up of building blocks (tiny, isolated, physical objects) was in grave doubt. The classical concept of a world of solid objects, governed by deterministic laws of nature, no longer made sense. Firstly, there was a strong sense of an 'alive' universe and, secondly, instead of being isolated, everything seemed to connect, interact, even interrelate!

THE QUANTUM WORLD VIEW

Quantum theory was not simply a new way of analysing heat radiation. In effect, it was a new *global* vision. In essence, it states that everything we perceive and experience is a great deal more than the initial, external impression we may obtain; that we experience life, not in isolated segments, but in *wholes* (quanta); that these 'lumps of experience' which impinge upon us are not inert, lifeless pieces of matter, but living energies; that our naming of the living reality we experience will at least be a probability-guess at what its real essence is (an essence best understood by interacting with it experimentally rather than trying to conceptualise it at an 'objective' distance).

A homely example of quantum theory is the wooden desk I use every day. Externally it seems to be a dead, inert, material object, which I can dismantle into its constituent parts and destroy if I wish. But if I take any fragment of the desk and place it under a very powerful microscope, I will notice that it is a sea bed of minute, 'moving' particles. Quantum theory tries to convince me that the desk is *alive*, although I can only observe this under the powerful microscope. The 'life' is crystallised in the timber, tightly packed and condensed, but comprising the same particles that make up my body and everything else in the universe.

The example of the alive desk may become somewhat more convincing when I consider its eventual demise. A time will come when the timber will rot and decay. Out of that 'dying' desk will emerge little creatures called *woodworm.* Where have they come from? From *within* the timber itself (although not

47

procreated by the timber). All these years, the woodworm have been 'existing' in a crystallised form within my desk, awaiting their hour of 'resurrection' (excuse the mixing of metaphors). They haven't been dead, though not 'alive' in the same sense as humans and other creatures we encounter in daily experience.

There is a real sense, therefore, in which my desk is *alive*, a pulsating collundrum of crystallised energy. Even the sweat, toil, devotion and creativity of those who made my desk belong to its essential nature, and may be having a minute but nonetheless real effect on my feelings and thinking as I write these words. My desk is a lump of living experience, which, at very fine and sensitive levels is affecting my psyche, just as I am affecting it.

Gary Zukav (1979, p.275) captivates something of the vibrancy and originality of quantum theory when he writes

> 'A quantum is a piece of action. The problem is that the quantum can be like a wave, and then again it can be like a particle, which is everything that a wave isn't. Furthermore, when a quantum is like a particle, it is not like a particle in the ordinary sense of the word. A subatomic "particle" is not a "thing" . . . A subatomic "particle" (quantum) is a set of relationships.'

Now that the deterministic nature of the classical paradigm had been seriously undermined, physicists found themselves grappling with concepts at one time considered to be the reserve of philosophy or religion. In 1927, Heisenberg formulated the *uncertainty principle*, noting that in our descriptions of atomic phenomena there are pairs of concepts (or aspects) which are interrelated, and precision in the definition of one concept is only possible with a measure of uncertainty in the other. About the same time, the Danish physicist, Niels Bohr introduced his notion of *complementarity* to explain something of the growing awareness within the scientific community that the universe was best understood as an interconnected web of relationships.

NEW LIGHT ON OLD CONCEPTS

At the beginning of this chapter, we outlined three dominant features of the classical world view: cause and effect; determinism; the whole equals the sum of the parts. In the quantum context, what do these terms mean?

1. **Cause and Effect:** In a quantum universe, all life is understood to function within one lump (quantum) of experience. Therefore, everything is affected (rather than caused) by everything else. The poet Francis Thompson captivated this view when he wrote: 'Thou cans't not stir a flower without disturbing a star.' (of which the butterfly effect may be a contemporary scientific example). At the observational level, my action of switching on the light may be described as cause and effect. Quantum theory invites (and challenges) me to the realisation that such an 'effect' is only possible in an electromagnetic universe; my ability to lift my hand in order to push the switch is also affected by the law of gravity. In other words, there is a great deal more to switching on the light bulb than mere cause and effect. In fact, 'cause and effect' has to do with the 'part' which can only be fully understood within the wider, global 'whole'.

That we are verging on mysticism and the spiritual scarcely needs acknowledging – and the pioneers of quantum theory readily recognised this. A real quantum scientist is not likely to have much of a problem with the following verse, in which (s)he may wish to substitute 'Life' for 'God':

> God sleeps in the stones,
> Dreams in the plants,
> Stirs in the animals
> And awakens in humanity.

(Source unknown)

2. **Determinism:** In a quantum universe, nothing is predictable, and the idea of life being in any way determined is abhorrent. Quantum theorists very much like the word 'probability'. Surprise, expectancy, wonder, creativity, beauty and elegance are the kind of words that enable the quantum scientist to make sense of reality.

There is a shadow side to this description which goes something like this: if the universe is not determined by an external agent (eg. God, as both Newton and Einstein believed) then we can begin determining and controlling it for our own self-aggrandisement. Let me emphasise: this is *not* quantum theory in its purity (if there is such a quality of theory); this is an aberration of what the original theorists conceived. Throughout the 1940s and 1950s it became the dominant orientation of the scientific and medical communities, and it still prevails, although its prevalence is beginning to wane in the face of recent scientific awareness and a growing wholistic consciousness.

In abandoning determinism, the perpetrators of the quantum theory were advocating a quality of mystical receptivity: be open to the unfolding (evolving) nature of life at all levels; life is not determined by blind, external forces – it is affected, for good or for bad, by the quality of our respect for its inherent processes, and our willingness to interact with (relate to) all life-forms in a gentle, non-exploitive, cooperative manner. Modern ecology, with its acute sense of planetary homoeostasis, is deeply in tune with the original dream of the quantum physicists.

3. **The whole equals the sum of the parts:** Although quantum theory is widely accepted in scientific circles, there are very few scientists who understand it fully, or who claim to be able to explain its nature simply and succinctly. I would submit that quantum theory is complex, but not necessarily complicated. The human body – a prime example of quantum theory at work – is highly complex, yet exhibits an amazing sense of order, rhythm and purpose.

What makes the human body special is the complex interaction of so many forces and energies that we do not (or cannot) observe in everyday life. There is no scientific, sociological or psychological means of measuring the intimacy and exhilaration of a young couple in the passion of courtship, in the eroticism of sexual embrace, in the ecstasy of contemplative prayer, in the gripping excitement of sport or achievement, in the placid serenity of a beautiful sunset, or alternatively, in the rending terror of pain and suffering, or the mental and physical exhaustion of agony and torture. In all these situations, and in many more besides, what is happening in the *whole* person can be neither analysed nor understood in terms of some or all of the *parts* of the human personality.

For the quantum theorists, the fact that the whole is greater than the sum of the parts underpins all reality. For everything in life, there is more to it than meets the eye. The real essence, the real meaning, dare we say, is deep within, which in practice, often means inside and outside the object we are observing.

In Chapter One, I examined the application of the wholistic vision to healthcare; here I reiterate that same example and explore its application to a healthy planet. With the rediscovery of psychosomatic medicine in the 1960s and 1970s, we began to understand anew not merely the nature of health but also the nature of the human personality. Health can be affected not merely by the mechanical functioning of the body itself, but by a vast array of extraneous factors, including environmental and psychological variables such as polluted surroundings, oppressive climate, hostile feelings from others, unsatisfactory relationships, inappropriate diet, work, rest, exercise. The health and wellbeing of a person depends on many agencies besides the human body.

And the same applies to Planet Earth. Politically, we have divided our earth into autonomous independent nations; we assume that if each one got its act together, then we would have harmony and prosperity on earth. That perception has really backfired. Not only have we a divided, polluted and exploited planet but, in most cases, nations themselves are struggling to live with some degree of dignity and inner harmony. The enterprise is failing (and will continue to fail) because we operate a faulty, inappropriate paradigm. The whole is greater than the sum of the parts; when we begin to think, act and plan *globally*, for the sake of the *whole,* then not merely will we create a better world, but national issues (such as the economy) will take on a significantly different meaning. Can we be sure we have never tried it? Perhaps it's about time we did! In fact, we may be approaching a time in world history where we have little choice other than to try it!

TWO SCIENTIFIC APPROACHES

CLASSICAL	QUANTUM
1. Determinstic.	Unpredictable – open to the unexpected.
2. Operates on the law of cause and effect.	Understands all interaction in terms of interdependence.
3. The whole equals the sum of the parts.	The whole is greater than the sum of the parts.
4. Things survive in mechanical isolation.	Everything is enriched by creative energy.
5. Matter is dead and inert.	Everything in the universe is alive.
6. We must keep pursuing the ultimate building blocks of matter.	There may be no ultimate building blocks in an alive universe.
7. Scientific experimentation is important.	Flowing with experience is important.
8. Life must be dissected and quantified in order to be understood.	Life comes to us in lumps (quanta) of experience.

NEGOTIATING THE SCIENTIFIC TRANSITION

Where are we then, in the transition from classical to quantum science? On the face of it, it would seem that the old classical model is as strong as it has ever been. In the Western world, everything is mechanised, structured, organised. Without a similar approach in parts of Africa and Latin America, it is hard to envisage any type of progress and development. The classical model has stood the test of time; it works! We cannot afford to part with it – and there is no fear that we will!

Despite its usefulness and utilitarian value, it has left our world in something of a polluted, exploited mess. Moreover, people in many of the rich nations are growing weary of the mechanisation. There is a psychological and spiritual emptiness, which often leads to feelings of alienation and depression, and to an increasing rate of compensatory and cheap thrills in alcohol, drugs, gambling or sex, not to mention the alarming rise in the number of suicides, especially in recent decades. For an increasing number, the mechanised world is a major source of disappointment, no longer producing the jobs that traditionally have provided security, status, achievement and money.

The classical model has served civilisation well, and is still immensely important. But it is inadequate for the emerging aspirations of humankind. In a world that has become a global village, people are moving (or in evolutionary terms, are being moved) beyond the nationalistic, parochial consciousness. Their thinking is expanding; their aspirations are for higher realities – not in another world, but in this one. Playing around with the 'parts' has little appeal for people who are fascinated by the 'whole'.

In the Western world, we have great difficulty in comprehending, never mind understanding, this transition. Our family upbringing, education and conditioning has strongly encouraged a sense of dependence on higher authorities. We look to parents, educators, State and Church officials for guidance; we grow up in the shadow of major institutions that inhibit our creativity and subvert our imaginations; we have been brainwashed in a classical value-system.

In the recent past, the quantum consciousness has tended to erupt outside rather than within familial, educational, State or Church contexts. The ecology movement has been one of its clearest statements, leading to protest currents such as CND, Greenpeace, Friends of the Earth, Globewatch etc. It is worthy of note that these groups are often accused of communist infiltration, a classic defence mechanism of the formal institutions.

53

Within the churches there has surfaced a whole range of alternative movements, in the form of sects, cults, and alternative communities. Some of these (notably the sects and cults) become even more rigid and destructive than the previous systems they tried to reform, but others (in particular the base communities) tend to adopt a highly creative and prophetic ambience. While base communities (as in Latin America) aim at closeness and intimacy in contradistinction to the anonymity and coldness of the big institution they often assume a socio-political orientation that gives them a distinctively global outlook. It is this unusual combination of the inner intimacy and the globally-based political vision that confirms the quantum identity.

From within the national institutions, the strongest sense of a quantum upheaval is occurring in the area of economics. Over the past twenty years, money has become global; in highly complex communication and computerised systems it travels hourly across the world, dipping into the major stock exchanges of London, New York and Tokyo. This 'invisible' money is what ultimately determines national strategies and financial planning. Because it is inherently invisible and global in nature, national governments are rapidly losing control over the world's financial situation, and this sense of panic, fear and uncertainty is often depicted in the major money markets in the face of unexpected monetary swings.

But nobody wishes to look at exactly what is happening; it is too threatening for the status quo! Instead, governments meddle around in short-term fiscal strategies, in an ever more difficult task of keeping the books balanced. After a while the money game becomes greedy, selfish and even bizarre. For financial rectitude, we build massive warehouses to store food; we pay grants to farmers to produce less; we even dump and destroy valuable produce – all in a world where one-third of humanity wallows in wealth while the remaining two-thirds macerate in a cesspool of disease and starvation. Not much quantum logic in all that!

But how long can it prevail? Isn't this type of short-sighted, utilitarian and grossly inhuman political strategy sounding the death knell for the classical world view? It has simply outgrown its usefulness. We need a new world vision, not the old mechanistic one which was essentially a strategy of divide and conquer, but a new, wholistic thrust challenging us to create a new world in the embrace of each other's arms – otherwise, we won't do it at all!

Bibliography:

Chopra, Deepak (1989), *Quantum Healing,* Bantam Books.

Davies, Paul C.W. (1988), *The Cosmic Blueprint,* Heinemann.

Hawking, Stephen (1988), *A Brief History of Time,* Bantam Books.

Sheldrake, Rupert (1988), *The Presence of the Past,* London: Collins.

Zukav, Gary (1980), *The Dancing Wu Li Masters: an Overview of the New Physics,* Fontana Books.

5

From Simplified to Integrated Spirituality

We are going to have to create a new language of prayer, and this new language of prayer has to come out of something which transcends all our traditions, and comes out of the immediacy of love.

Thomas Merton.

Thus far, we have explored worldly issues and some readers may be surprised to see spirituality raising its head. After all, spiritual matters have to do with the church, and since that has little relevance for most of us these days, what's the point in dragging it in?

An interesting feature of the mechanistic mind-set is the tendency to work from without and move inwards. We look for all the *facts*, the hard data, observations that can be checked and verified. Issues that cannot be explained in terms of the facts, we choose to ignore or dismiss, or we postpone them, hoping they will make factual sense at a later stage. Progressively we begin to understand the inner nature of life, but only as far as scientific and verifiable information will carry us. Anything beyond the hard facts is considered spurious and ultimately unreal.

Applied to *machines*, it makes a good deal of sense, but not to social systems, such as a nation, a factory or a school, and less so to human beings. In the realm of human behaviour, observations based on hard facts can be so grossly misleading. Often they fail to unearth or reveal the real reasons (the motivation, impulse, desire etc.) that drive people to behave in certain ways, individually or collectively.

This deeper realm of the human psyche – which, I submit, is also an aspect of social systems and even of material creation – is what I call *spirituality*. In its wholistic sense, it has nothing to do with churches, rituals or religions. It is a quality of inner experience shared by all people and unique to each person. Its focal point in human behaviour is *the search for meaning* which each person pursues in the depth of his or her own heart and which we humans articulate collectively in a vast range of social and ritual behaviours.

The transition being explored in this chapter is about the shift from a spirituality almost exclusively focused on formal religion and church allegiance to one that is outgrowing the need for that exclusive frame of reference. In the simplified version, spirituality and religion were deemed to be the same thing, and religion implied allegiance to one or other denominational church. It was a simple, mechanical arrangement of spirituality-religion-church, buttressed with a specific, institutional framework, strong leadership from the top, and clear-cut, black-and-white rules and regulations. Islam and Roman Catholicism still retain strong elements of this outdated model.

It may be compared to family upbringing in the traditional Western household. Children's lifestyle and behaviour tend to be highly structured and organised under vigilant and caring parental eyes. In one sense, children need this infrastructure if they are to attain inner strength and security to confront the adult world. If this same lifestyle is imposed right through adolescence and young adulthood, not merely does it invite reaction and rebellion, but it jeopardises the young person's hope of coming to grips with the reality of adult life. The simplified version of childhood formation has to be outgrown so that the young adult can begin to integrate the diverse experiences encountered in the adult world.

Simplified spirituality tends to be one of superficial rules and regulations. External behaviour tends to be overrated, while internal motivation is poorly understood. Formal teachings over-emphasise some aspects of life to the detriment of others, eg. sexual morality in Roman Catholicism, monotheism in Islam. Phrases like, 'The only important thing is to ... (obey the Pope; remain faithful to the *Sharia*)' tend to be used rather glibly and freely.

THE INTEGRATED APPROACH

In the integrated approach, we transcend the idea of one thing being more important than all others; *everything* is considered to be *relatively* important. Spirituality is not just about religion, or church attendance, or fidelity to one or other legal requirement. Spirituality is understood to be an innate wisdom of the human heart that enlivens a zest for life, a search for meaning and purpose, a love for all that is good and beautiful, a passion to create a better world, a sensitivity to the life-energy (God, if you wish) that permeates the entire cosmos.

How people activate and articulate this inner wisdom is one of the most urgent questions of our time. In the past, it was perceived to be the challenge of home and school for youth; church and faith-community for adults. It is clear that all these institutions are failing dismally, still inculcating a value-system that belongs largely to the older model.

In the Western world, there has been a mass apostasy from formal religions. There is no indication that a new religion is likely to be born. So where is the spiritual energy being channelled? In many cases, it is redirected into the 'false Gods' of power, property, wealth, exploitation of the Earth or the several forms of inordinate pleasure such as alcohol, drugs, gambling and sex. These are the areas in which people seek (and to some extent find) meaning and purpose in life. At the end of the day, this pleasure/power instinct becomes a death-wish, as Freud indicated so succinctly many years ago. Could it be that coronary ailments, alcoholism, drug abuse, AIDS are the cultural death-wishes of our time?

In a sense we know the problem, but we become extremely shortsighted when it comes to proposing a solution or resolution to the dilemma. We assume that a revival of religion and a restoration of disciplined morality, more laws and stronger leadership from the top will restore 'law and order'. We apply ointment to a wound that is essentially cancerous. Only major surgery will remedy the defect.

In this time of transition, the old world order is in decline, decay and chaos. Even our most cherished and sacred institutions are heading for disintegration. Religions and churches are losing the people, with the notable exception of Islam, which is expanding on the gullibility of disenchanted youth, swelling the numbers of a religion that is increasingly becoming a blind and irrational ideology. People are becoming less religious *but not less spiritual.* The spiritual problem of our age is that most people are out of tune with their innate, spiritual selves, some because of the agnosticism and spiritual indifference of our time, but others (perhaps the majority) because their real spiritual potential has been misguided through religious indoctrination.

The challenge for the future is to restore something of the integrated nature of spiritual growth, to help us humans to reconnect with our inner capacity for mystery, beauty, harmony, order, love and God, and rediscover the spiritual power which animates and sustains all life in the universe. This new spiritual sense is being rekindled, not in the religions and churches where we would expect it to happen, but among psychologists, who probe the inner (human) depths, and by physicists who probe the inner (cosmological) realm. If spirituality is to survive this transition – and I believe it certainly will – it may be the prophets outside our churches who will become the saviours of humankind.

INCLUSIVE SPIRITUALITY

A spirituality of integration considers everything in the world to be relatively important. Nothing in life is too banal, materialistic, secular or unspiritual to be included. And old dualisms of God v Man, Earth v Heaven, Spiritual v Secular, Sin v Grace are considered to be superficial and simplistic. In a wholistic universe, everything is *one.* Unity and harmony are the underlying energies and also the ultimate goal. Fragmentation and disintegration exist on the surface. They must be taken seriously and respected for what they are. Yet they are superficial, inappropriate, 'sinful' aspects of an evolving and unfolding universe. For the spiritually versatile, they are the challenges that call forth growth in care, compassion, concern, justice and, ultimately, human and global transformation.

The integrated perspective is one of involvement and participation. Politics and religion are man-made constructs, dualistic labels that fragment the one experience of life in which everybody participates, consciously or otherwise. In this spiritual orientation, God is not a figure in the clouds, nor merely the personified Messiah of one or all the great religions. God permeates all life and yet transcends all reality. God is something much more real than even the most sacred categories of the formal religions.

In the integrated approach, our call is not to obey or worship God, but to participate in the spiritual unfolding of universal life. We are co-creators with a creative God. We are people with a dark and sinful side to our personalities; with nature we share in the groaning and struggle for our final evolutionary liberation. Life will not condemn us for our greed and selfishness, unless of course, we condemn ourselves by wallowing in our misery or gloating in our exploitation of self and others. But that is not integrated behaviour! Life (God) has endowed us with the inner strength and outer resources to grow beyond our destructive tendencies and become enlightened, liberated people. This is the task of an entire lifetime, a spiritual journey we share with the whole of creation, unfolding into the eternal destiny of God.

COPING WITH TRANSITION

We live in an age of spiritual ferment. People worship many Gods, most of them false, including the fabricated deities of many religions. As human beings, we need our idols, our images and fantasies. In all our lives, however, there are those times of transition to let go of the old props and move into a new and risky space. We adopt new images, maybe even new idols. But each new experience deepens our grasp of reality, and hopefully, we come a little closer to the truth which enlightens the mind and opens the heart to the great mystery of universal life.

This is something of the spiritual pilgrimage of our time.

TWO STRANDS OF SPIRITUALITY

SIMPLIFICATION	INTEGRATION
1. Dualistic (either/or).	Complementary (both/and).
2. Keep things as simple as possible.	Life is innately complex.
3. 'The only important thing is . . .'	Everything is relatively important.
4. Get down to the essentials	The non-essentials are also important.
5. Preserve the good; eliminate evil.	Try and hold the two together – both represent life.
6. Change the external behaviour.	Get to the source of the problem.
7. Adopt the quickest solution.	'Things take time.'
8. We need authority to maintain equilibrium.	We need everybody's participation to integrate complexity.

Gone are the old certainties, the time when things were plain and simple. We live in an universe of expanding complexity (explored in Part Two). We need a spirituality that will enable us to find our feet in the diversity and chaos of our age. We need a spiritual vision that will enable us to hold, not a few, but many issues in perspective. We need open minds and expanded hearts to comprehend something of the length and breadth, the height and depth of the mystery of life. We need to transcend the old barriers of creed and denomination, so that we can find the common language to embark on this wholistic, spiritual enterprise that touches the core of meaning in every person today.

The practical implications of this challenge are being worked out in a scattered and disconnected range of experiments, some within formal religions, most of them outside the established creeds. The rediscovery of Eastern meditation offers some promising possibilities as does the rediscovery of creation-centred spirituality in the West, celebrating the sacredness of the earth and the inter-dependence of all life-forms in our universe. But the spiritual consciousness may have to become a good deal more turbulent before we open to its challenge – and that may happen sooner than most of us anticipate!

Bibliography:

Fox, Matthew (1984), *Original Blessing: A Primer in Creation Spirituality,* New Mexico: Bear & Co. Inc.

Goleman, Daniel (1988), *The Meditative Mind,* Los Angeles: J.P. Tarcher.

Hay, David (1982), *Exploring Inner Space,* Mowbrays.

6

From Independent to Interdependent Interaction

Synthesis and pattern-seeing are survival skills for the twenty-first century.

Marilyn Ferguson

A feature of the mechanistic consciousness, dominating the Western world in particular since the late seventeenth century, was a tendency to think of everything as isolated, autonomous and self-contained. Atoms, as the basic units of matter, were considered indivisible and indestructible (hence the term elementary particles). Even the splitting of the atom at the beginning of the present century did not undermine the conviction that life thrived on the autonomy and individuality of the many parts comprising the whole.

A similar consciousness prevailed in the political and religious spheres. National autonomy has long been accepted as a basic right, and the achievement of independence by African nations in the 1960s was hailed as a huge step forward for the freedom and progress of the African people. Prior to the 1960s, religious dialogue, exchanging views and experiences, was practically unknown. Within Christianity, denominations kept well apart, and even protected their independence with well-defined rules and regulations.

And, of course, this sense of independence was largely generated by human beings themselves. Man was master of creation, the world was to be conquered and controlled. Human beings exert a quality of control and autonomy, often at the expense of other life-forms, even at the expense of their own species, eg. men have produced a cultural stereotype which, even to this day, subjects women into a more subservient role. Political, social and religious systems have validated and affirmed this male superiority.

INDEPENDENCE AND INDIVIDUALITY

And finally, there is the independence of the individual person himself/herself, deemed to be one of the most fundamental values of society. Personal freedom and autonomy are considered essential to the development of mature adulthood within the political and social systems of our world. Occasionally this leads to exaggerated individualism, whereby the person procures the fulfilment of his or her own needs at the expense of others. It was to undermine this creeping and dangerous trend that communism was invented; where successful, as in the Soviet Union, it stripped people not merely of their autonomy but of all that made them human.

In contemporary Western society, individuality is cherished and safeguarded. The basic emphasis is on the value of the person above and beyond the group, the social system and creation at large. Humans, as individuals, are deemed to be supreme, just as God is supreme over creation. Statements like: 'The person is all that matters'; 'Humans come first' or 'People are more important than things' all belong to this category.

In an effort to assert the absolute sacredness of the person, individuality veers towards a form of superiority which is both subtle and dangerous. The tendency to juxtapose the individual to everything else in creation can easily lead to exploitive and manipulative abuses of other life-forms, inanimate objects and, indeed, other people. It leads to forms of fragmentation which militate against wholism.

What initially seems to be a very coherent and humane concept can easily become devious and destructive. Western democracies pride themselves in safeguarding individuality; so do the multinationals! This has led to an exaggerated self-concept, very different from individualism, but ultimately no less lethal and destructive.

Individuality is also a concept warmly cherished by the Christian churches. The supremacy of God is a prerequisite for the supremacy of man, which in turn validates categories of leadership at various organisational levels of society, eg. Pope, Cardinals, Bishops, Clergy; or politically, Prime Minister and a host of elected representatives at different levels. What we have created in the name of democracy – in order to safeguard human individuality – has, in recent times, led to many subtle forms of subversion and corruption. At the end of the day, nature has been polluted, other life-forms have been brutalised, and even humans themselves have been degraded.

CHIEF FEATURES OF TWO SYSTEMS

INDEPENDENCE	INTERDEPENDENCE
1. Everything survives on its own strength.	Everything needs everything else to survive meaningfully.
2. Man is alone before God.	As a social, spiritual creature, no person is ever alone.
3. Man is supreme over nature.	Humans are called to be stewards of creation, befriending Mother Earth in her growth and development.
4. Individual identity and autonomy is important.	We discover our true identity in partnership and in community.
5. Private property must be safeguarded.	All people are entitled to an equal share of the goods of creation.
6. 'Divide and conquer'.	'Live and let live'.

7. National independence is essential for peace on earth.	Nations are merely a human, political construct, one that is becoming increasingly problematic.
8. If governments cooperate, we can solve all global problems.	We need a global government, because most contemporary problems are global in nature.

THE SHIFT TOWARDS INTERDEPENDENCE

For many people, interdependence is still quite a novel idea. It asserts that nothing – from the atom to the person, to the nation to the universe – exists or makes sense in isolation. Everything in the universe is interconnected, impinges upon everything else, and is dependent on all other life-forms for survival and fulfilment. Everything needs everything else.

Interdependence is not a new idea. In prehistoric societies, it was an unquestioned assumption; all life-forms enjoyed a degree of uniqueness and autonomy, but their ultimate value rested in their ability to enrich and complement one another. It was the agricultural revolution in the tenth century BC that undermined an otherwise wholistic vision, creating the competitive and exploitive differentiation that has bedevilled civilisation ever since.

Ecologists and environmentalists are among the first to resurrect the ancient wisdom of interdependence. Throughout the 1960s and 1970s, we have recaptured a great deal of lost wisdom on the delicate and magnificent balance within the ecosystem. Our environment is an interconnected web of relationships wherein each life-form discovers its true identity, not in independent isolation, but in interdependent cooperation with all other aspects of the environment.

Ecologically, we humans are the great offenders; we have veered off on a tangent of our own, exploiting the ecosystem as if it was an object to be controlled and conquered. We fail to recall the sobering fact that we are rather recent visitors to Planet Earth, where life has flourished for billions of years in a vast and diverse array without our assistance. Our very survival is dependent on the existence of all other life-forms. Exterminate any one – animals, birds, fish, even insects – and our survival would be seriously threatened. *We* need all other life-forms, but in evolutionary terms, they do not need us; they flourished without us in the past and presumably could do so again!

By wrecking our planet as we recklessly do – denuding our forests, polluting our lakes, rivers and seas, exterminating some life species, depleting the ozone layer – we are, most of all, exploiting ourselves. Planet Earth has a strange and powerful resilience, precisely because it possesses an innate ability to function interdependently. It is we humans who are out of step with the creative process, and it is we who are likely to perish because of our greedy and reckless manipulation.

Even in the event of a nuclear holocaust, the heaviest loser would be human beings themselves. Given a few hundred years – a mere second in the evolutionary timescale – Planet Earth would revive again and recommence the cycle and variety of life-forms. At the end of the day humans cannot conquer the earth, less so destroy it. Our only mature and meaningful response is to learn to live in harmony with the planet, and with the wider cosmos in which life has placed us.

NATION STATES OR INTERNATIONAL COMMUNITY

These reflections lead us to consider the other great resistance of our evolutionary development: the fragmentation of the earth into empires and nations. As already noted, the division of the Earth into parts to be fought for, conquered and owned, is the byproduct of the agricultural revolution. Perhaps it was a necessary, temporary development, appropriate for the evolutionary consciousness of the time, but it has clearly outlived its usefulness and threatens any sane and sustainable future we try to make possible for the Earth's five billion people.

The problems facing humankind today – especially the massive injustices that polarise our world into haves and have-nots – is a *global* issue demanding *global* solutions. While national governments continue to compete with one another, while the rich North continues to exploit the impoverished South, while hungry power-seekers of East and West play infantile war-games, as in the Gulf war of 1991, there is no hope of addressing the crucial issues confronting humankind today. Even if the international debt of Third World nations was wiped out; even if Western nations doubled their aid to poorer countries, it would have little impact on the overall wellbeing of humanity.

Sooner or later we must, on an international scale, transcend the 'them and us' mentality. Our Earth is one; ecologically, it functions as a single organism with a magnificent and mysterious interplay of life and energy (the Gaia hypothesis initially propounded by James Lovelock and Lynn Margullis, and now adopted by an increasing number of scientists). Economically, we still maintain national currencies and a superficial semblance of economic independence but, in fact, money has become a global, international reality, a type of universal 'energy' which circulates round the globe via international telex and electronic communication systems, dipping into the big money markets of London, Tokyo and New York. It is this invisible, economic 'energy' that controls the financial destiny of every national government; and, confronted with this reality, national governments have little control over their financial affairs.

Governments continue to plan on the basis of a competitive world market. The great injustice of our time is that an increasing number of nations, both North and South, are unable to enter this cut-throat and highly sophisticated racketeering. The multinationals and the rich nations have engineered a trade pact that enables the rich to become richer while the poor grow poorer.

Perhaps the saddest element of this grossly outrageous scenario is that we set in motion some forty years ago the machinery to outgrow this national greed and the self-aggrandisement that has led to our present problems. I am referring to the United Nations, that supreme international group of some 160 nation-states, established to symbolise and forward the move towards a new community of all Earth's citizens. Sadly, it has become little more than an international gossip club. It is devoid of any real power and seems unable to assume the role of international stewardship which, theoretically, is its primary function. Nonetheless, its very existence, and its survival over the past forty years, is a powerful reminder to humankind that, sooner or later, the creation of a world government is possible. Then, and only then, will we fully appreciate our new found sense of interdependence.

With the developments of the recent past in trans-international travel and communication, the Earth has become small and intimate. The global village is no longer a Marshall McLuhan fantasy. The consciousness has changed, but the structural reality has remained essentially the same: individuals pursuing selfish goals in self-centred, profit-making enterprises, in an international competitive market where individual states often act like savage predators, ravaging a fragile creature called Mother Earth.

It all seems so wrong, and so ridiculous! And it looks as if it will take something of a global catastrophe to effect the transition I describe, and thus correct the imbalance and gross injustice. What that might entail is what I attempt to unravel in Part Two of this book.

Bibliography:

Bohm, David & Feat, F. David (1987), *Science, Order and Creativity,* Bantam Books.

Lovelock, James (1979), *Gaia: A New Look at Life on Earth,* Oxford University Press.
(1988), *The Ages of Gaia,* Oxford University Press.

Sahtouris, Elisabet (1989), *Gaia: The Human Journey from Chaos to Cosmos,* London & New York: Pocket Books.

PART TWO

CHAOS AND CREATIVITY

In November, 1988, British television's Channel Four produced a documentary entitled *The Science of Chaos*. It was based on an intriguing study by journalist James Gleick (1988) in which we read:

> 'Now that science is looking, chaos seems to be everywhere . . . Chaos breaks across the lines that separate scientific disciplines. Because it is a science of the global nature of systems, it has brought together thinkers from fields that had been widely separated . . . The most passionate advocates of the new science go so far as to say that twentieth-century science will be remembered for just three things: relativity, quantum mechanics and chaos.'
>
> (pp. 5-6)

CHAOTIC ORDER

Throughout the 1980s, physicists, biologists, astronomers and economists have created a new way of understanding the growth of complexity in nature. Gone are the days when the 'isolated building blocks' were the main target of research and exploration. We now acknowledge that our universe cannot be broken down into a few simple, elementary units of matter. Not alone is that ultimate simplicity based on false assumptions, but it undermines the very creativity of life which makes complexity essential, and not merely complexity, but chaos as well.

In classical science chaos was attributed to 'randomness', a freak of nature that science might one day understand and

73

control. Classic examples of chaotic behaviour include the dripping of a water tap, the turbulence of a river, the design of snowflakes, the unpredictability of weather, the fibrillation of the human heart. Now that chaotic systems are being mathematically modelled, we are discovering hidden patterns of order and beauty embedded in the chaos; eg. we can actually measure very rugged coastlines with the aid of a new branch of maths called *fractals* (cf. Mandelbrot, 1977).

What, in fact, is happening is this: advocates of many scientific disciplines are acknowledging that our universe – at all levels of life – has a strange and amazing propensity that often comes to light most elegantly in dealing with irregularities and chaotic behaviour. It is as if the chaos is the precondition for launching the entire system into a whole new way of being.

Such observations open up new marvels about the universe in which we live. Foremost among these is the so-called *butterfly effect*. Interdependence within universal life is so widespread and sensitive that the beating of the butterfly's wings can alter the course of a tornado on the other side of the world. The interplay of chance and law powerfully affects all life around us. This was ably demonstrated by Aspect's experiment in 1982, when two identical photons were emitted in opposite directions by a calcium atom; it was noted that if certain influences were brought to bear on one of the photons, then the second is also affected, although the latter may be on the other side of the moon. What an universe to be alive in!

CREATIVE COMPLEXITY

In Part Two of this book we continue to explore aspects of the current transition, focussing more explicitly on the movement from the old, linear, mechanical simplicity to the emerging new, non-linear, wholistic complexity. What I wish to highlight is that the transition will produce a lot of chaos and confusion, and that it is precisely in this 'destructive' and 'negative' unfolding that we must be alert for the seeds of life and creativity.

Our upbringing and education have seriously diminished

our ability to utilise chaos creatively. We just bury the negative by denial and projection. We run away from pain and discomfort. Our compulsion to control and manipulate shortcircuits our experience of so many things in life. We fail to experience reality in the fullness of the Yin-Yang spectrum. Consequently, our perceptions tend to be partial, often extremely narrow and utilitarian, making our subsequent response only partially appropriate, if indeed, appropriate at all!

All indications are that we are moving into an era of expanded horizons, into an evolutionary phase in which traditional, dualistic distinctions become irrelevant and, maybe, meaningless. The initial studies on the science of chaos reveal a fascinating interdependence between order and chaos, complexity and simplicity. One aspect can trigger off the other for a whole variety of reasons, most of which we do not understand. Interference, with a view to manipulating and controlling, is becoming increasingly inappropriate and counterproductive.

We seem to be moving towards a new, mystical horizon where those who are prepared to 'be still and wait' have the greatest chance, not merely of surviving, but of participating in the unfolding cosmic process. The compulsive work-aholics, the masters of our high-tech world, have so much to let go of! Only a profound conversion of mind and heart will enable us to reach this promised, risky land!

Bibliography:

Gleick, James (1988), *Chaos: Making a New Science,* London: Heinemann.

Handy, Charles (1990), *The Age of Unreason,* Arrow Books.

Mandelbrot, Benoit (1977), *The Fractal Geometry of Nature,* New York: W H Freeman & Co.

7

From Institutional to Networking Structures

> *Often a revolution has an interdisciplinary character; its central discoveries often come from people straying outside the normal bounds of their specialities.*
>
> James Gleick

During the Second World War, petrol was rationed in many European countries and regular car-users had to resort to walking or cycling. In an attempt to create adequate bicycle space, one London hospital suggested that each staff member using a bicycle sign a 'bicycle book' on entering the hospital. In a few weeks, management would then know how much 'parking' space was needed for the bicycles and would provide it according to demand.

That happened in 1946. Thirty years later, hospital staff using bicycles were still signing the book. Some asked why, got no satisfactory answer, and continued to obey the system. And Fred, the desk porter at the main entrance, ensured that the procedure was followed. He inherited the custom from his predecessor and had kept it up faithfully for twelve years.

Why? 'I was told it was one of my duties, and I just do what I'm told.' But when in 1979 the local health authority ordered an evaluation of the hospital services – with a view to reducing the workforce (among other things) – Fred found himself challenged with questions which proved not merely embarrassing but quite threatening for the security of his job. Fred now found himself also asking: 'Why are they signing this bicycle book?' It took him some time to discover that it was a ritual that had long outlived its time, and served no purpose other than to waste money, time and energy.

WHAT IS AN INSTITUTION?

This anecdote, silly and stupid though it may seem, is typical of what institutionalisation is about. An institution can be any system or organisation in which people interact. The family, a golf club, a factory, a school, a nation, the Vatican, the United Nations are all institutions. Despite significant differences in purpose and in their mode of operation, they all contain subtle and powerful elements which society largely takes for granted.

We assume – and quite rightly – that humans are social creatures who need various forms of social organisation in order to function meaningfully and effectively in society. Many different sciences – sociological and religious – consider the family to be the basic social unit of society; as such, we consider the family to be above the scrutiny and evaluation we deem appropriate for other social institutions such as a school, a factory or a voluntary organisation. By and large, we turn a blind eye to the fact that the nuclear family (father, mother and two children) is no longer the norm in contemporary Western society; even marriage itself is undergoing something of a transition.

At the other end of the spectrum is the complex institution called the nation state, under the control and leadership of national government, democratically elected by the people (in most cases). Once again, we assume this structure to be normative and essential to the progress of Planet Earth. Few people realize that national governments today are quite helpless at the hands of international forces, particularly economic ones. Nor are national governments acting in isolation capable of addressing the economic, environmental (ecological) and commercial issues confronting humankind today. As our world grows in its sense of internationality and globality, nationalism becomes increasingly inept, archaic and irrelevant.

Among the transitions taking place in today's world is a shift from the exclusive focus on institutions – as being the norm for social and political organisation – to new and, as yet, poorly organised, alternative structures which seek to connect people with their social and political environment. This new infrastructure we call *networking,* and its evolving nature we explore later in this chapter.

WHY ARE INSTITUTIONS FAILING?

Why are institutions falling into disrepute? Probably because they cannot imbibe and accommodate the emerging global (wholistic) consciousness of our time. Why not? Because, perhaps, *they were never intended to.* Most of the major institutions we know today – ones we assume to have existed from time immemorial – are relatively recent phenomena. Marriage, as an institution based on the lifelong commitment: 'Till death do us part' is very much an invention of the seventeenth and eighteenth centuries, when its primary goal was perceived to be the procreation of children and when most adults didn't live beyond fifty years of age. Even the more recent image of the nuclear family has outgrown that initial understanding.

The traditional institution of marriage simply cannot contain the new consciousness in which:

a) Sexuality is perceived to be a dimension of intimacy, whether within or outside marriage;
b) People live up to seventy, maybe eighty years of age, in a world of great social mobility, where lifelong attachments are no longer necessarily perceived to be life-enhancing;
c) The concept of intimate partnerships is being extended to include one-parent families, homosexual unions and other forms of close affiliation.

The Christian churches and other faiths, such as Islam, frequently bemoan the fact that the family (and marriage) is 'under attack' from the 'evil' forces at work in society. This is a rather emotionally – and morally laden – accusation that very likely misses the real issue(s). It is a superficial judgment of a changing, complex, global situation. All contemporary institutions are battling, not just for survival, but for a rediscovery of their *raison d'être.* Even if we assume that they are 'under attack' – a conviction I personally do not share – their progressive fragmentation is activated as much by *internal malaise* as by external attack.

Most of the institutions that form the infrastructure of today's world, politically, socially, economically and ecclesiastically, belong to the old order in which the *machine* was the leading paradigm. As institutions, they sought to hold together in *balance* and *control* the parts that made up the 'mechanical' unit. To do this they created strong, top-down authoritarian leaderships. Control was the leading metaphor; balance, the supreme virtue and conflict the great vice.

The story of the bicycle book at the beginning of this chapter illustrates both the strength and weakness of the institutional model. The emphasis lay heavily on control and manipulation of the individual parts on the assumption that the smooth running of each part guaranteed the effective functioning of the whole organism. What often happened was that one part did not know what the other was doing. Services were unnecessarily duplicated, resources unnecessarily wasted, and excessive costs were incurred. Worst of all, there was little or no creative interaction or cooperation among the personnel of the different 'parts'. The mechanistic *raison d'être* determined the quality and quantity of all activity. Little wonder that business enterprises had to undergo such a massive overhaul throughout the 1970s and 1980s to compete and function more effectively in the contemporary world.

As a model, this quality of institution has served us well. Despite its limitations, it was probably right for its time and is still a *valid* way of organising our world at the different levels we referred to earlier. It's not that the model is wrong; it is more a case of it being *unsuited,* indeed *irrelevant,* to the emerging consciousness. Our world is calling out for social structures that will be more fluid and flexible, more open-ended and mobile, more creative and adventuresome, less self-reliant and more interdependent in their basic orientation, and, above all, more global in their ambience.

WHAT IS NETWORKING?

The practical challenges of this new vision are beginning to

79

take shape in all types of clumsy and controversial ways and, by and large, outside rather than within the orthodox setting of Church or State. One conceptual framework in which we try to make sense of the new orientations is that of *networking*.

Because of its multifaceted nature, networking is not a neatly definable entity. Naisbitt (1982, p.197) identifies three fundamental reasons why networks have become important in our time: (a) the death of traditional structures; (b) the din of information overload, and (c) the past failures of hierarchies. It is easier to define what networking does rather than what it is. Lipnack & Stamps (1986, p.4) provide a good working definition:

> 'Nowhere is the use of the words *network* and *networking* more prevalent than in the computer world: the large, centralised behemoths that ruled the electronic world of only a few years past are now encircled by decentralized nets of small autonomous microcomputers.
>
> '. . . In the end, it is the sense of cooperation among self-reliant, decision-making peers that visualises a network. Networking swallows up buck passing and renders each of us more responsible, self-respecting and creative. The process of networking itself changes those who are networked, by expanding each person's matrix of connections.'

Networking is a wholistic concept that nurtures a number of processes otherwise considered to be independent and autonomous functions. People begin to link up with a whole range of others, irrespective of background, expertise or the traditional distinctions of race, creed or colour of skin; people link up because the linking itself is somehow felt to be the right thing to do. And this is no childish pursuit of security through numerical strength, nor is it an escapist tendency, hoping to get lost in a 'friendly' crowd.

A group of people may gather round an environmental issue such as a locally polluted lake, or a social issue such as poor housing. No longer do we think of going directly to the person or people officially responsible for these areas of concern, because in the complicated bureaucracy of contemporary life it is often unclear who precisely is responsible, and, secondly, because of the cumbersome nature of modern political institutions, often strangulated by red tape, one is never sure if one's complaint has been received, never mind responded to. The local pressure group (which, in fact, is a great deal more than a 'pressure' group) is likely to have a much more effective impact.

What is of significance in such groups is the quality of bonding and interaction that takes place. Traditional class distinctions are often superseded: the local doctor, housewife and unemployed person become colleagues around. a common cause. A new sense of neighbourliness and befriending ensues. Each becomes aware of the limitations of trying to go it alone, whereas the strength in numbers brings reassurance and some semblance of hope.

As the network takes on an identity of its own, the actual issue that brought the group together may become secondary, while the sense of people power assumes the primary role. As Naisbitt (1982 p.197) reminds us: 'Networks fulfil the high-touch needed for belonging.' Individuals begin to realize that their specific contribution, which carries little weight by going it alone, becomes as significant as any other contribution within the networking structure. The network will often draw forth the shy and reserved in a manner that rarely happens in hierarchical institutions, whose major 'crime' is the creation of *dependency*. To quote Naisbitt once more: 'In the network environment, rewards come by empowering others, not by climbing over them.' (1982, p.204). In the networking environment, participation becomes the governing principle; imagination and initiative are considered to be the supreme virtues. The root metaphor is that of a tapestry, and even conflict is deemed to be creative and productive.

As a network coheres, and people share their ideas and resources, a creativity from within can begin to unfold. No longer is the group satisfied with registering its protest about pollution, housing, women's rights etc. Frequently, the group will veer towards exploring strategies for action; rather than waiting on the 'powers that be', the network opts for its own remedial action, which often will be perceived as (and, in fact, may well be) subversive and, therefore, a threat to the official powers. A timely and controversial example is that of the women's movement within both church and society in general.

THE NETWORKING HORIZON

Is the network some new type of institution? It could become yet another institution, and if it does it is no longer a network. To be effective, a network must have a structure, but the healthy network keeps this structure as loose, fluid and flexible as possible. What tends to happen, therefore, is that *networks begin networking with each other.* And this is what makes the concept so exciting and potentially relevant and appropriate for the emerging consciousness of our age.

In its essential nature, a network veers towards expanded horizons. Lipnack and Stamps (1986, p.148) captivate something of this orientation when they write:

> 'Networks work because of the dynamic relation-ships that transpire among the people involved. To understand the process of networking, we have to shift from thinking about *things* and the way they are built, to thinking about *relationships* and the way they behave.'

Today, information, which was at one time the reserve of an enlightened intelligentsia, is now the shared possession of all humankind. At this level, power has been taken from the powerful and shared with all, including the powerless. The powerful now feel stripped, and react either defensively (with the politics of 'law and order'), or assertively (trying to reinforce so-called democracy). Mainstream Western politics – especially of the capitalist brand – is a threatened species, a fact that is reflected in the increasing tendency to disown the political system: only half the American electorate turned out for the last two presidential elections, not a symptom of apathy (I suggest) but one of subversive protest.

The global networking which has grown up around the sharing of information moves to the next stage: strategies to translate the new consciousness into liberating action. While nation-states continue the outdated political game of isolated self-government, it is becoming blatantly obvious that the major issues confronting humanity today – poverty, injustice, racism, terrorism, environmental pollution, use of natural resources, economic debt – can only be addressed *globally*, not nationally. The consciousness is ripe; surely, the action must be imminent:

> 'We are stuck at the nation-state level of human organisation. World order is not emerging from alliances of nations, which are notoriously fragile and incomplete. Rather . . . thousands of subnational organisations are forming multinational associations and creating an increasingly interdependent web of international corporate, institutional and professional relationships that are not directly dependent on national governments. That is, we are not moving directly from national to international government but, rather, are detouring through earlier subnational stages in order to re-form at a higher transnational level.'
>
> (Lipnack & Stamps, 1986, pp.176-177)

It is extremely difficult to communicate verbally or in written form what networking is about. It is essentially an experimental mode, whose credibility is only compelling with hindsight. Because of the breakdown of traditional patriarchy and the inability of current hierarchical structures to address creatively the major (global) issues of our time, the rank and file are abandoning – subconsciously rather than consciously – the mainstream institutions. Even where circumstances force people to stick with such institutions, eg. our dependence on the health or social services, people are rapidly losing faith in such services. They avail themselves of them, not because they perceive them to be valuable, but simply because they have nowhere else to turn.

STRUCTURE: TWO DIFFERENT MODELS

INSTITUTIONAL	NETWORKING
1. Powerful and centrally controlled.	Diffuse without a central authority.
2. Apparently strong and enduring.	Apparently too diffuse to be effective.
3. Self-perpetuating.	Tends to dissolve or reorganise in serving people's needs.
4. Controlled from above.	Animated from within.
5. Legally based and officially structured.	Loosely structured, with a minimum of rules.
6. Thrives on specialisation.	Thrives on diversity of gifts and talents.
7. There are standard modes of procedure – no risk-taking.	Emphasis is on creativity and cooperation; after that, trust the process.
8. Resists change.	Thrives on change and feels at home with it.
9. People are useful as 'functionaries' to serve the outfit.	People are cherished for their giftedness.
10. Labour-intensive; everybody has an assigned task.	Things happen through creative interaction; difficult to say who initiates what.

NETWORKS ARE SUBVERSIVE

Out of this sense of frustration and desperation is emerging the alternative consciousness that is birthing the phenomenon we call *networking*. It is very much a struggle of powerless people trying to empower each other, because the major institutions, initially created to serve their needs, now undermine their dignity and value as people. The institutions have become self-perpetuating and have lost touch with their original purpose. The people have no choice but to move in another direction.

Accusations of betrayal and subversion are readily forthcoming. Quite simply this indicates that the institution is on the defensive; it is beginning to feel its own vulnerability and yet is unable to face it. Networks *are* subversive; they articulate a whole new way of doing things. Their agenda is not the destruction of institutions but the creation of a new space to answer fundamental needs.

The fact that the 'new is elsewhere' is not the result of a carefully planned strategy, but the outcome of the creative imagination when the human spirit is pushed to its limits. When the old order collapses into disarray, as is happening extensively today, the ensuing chaos has a strange sense of creativity, a type of quantum leap that defies disintegration. It is a transition for which there is no known rationale other than that mysterious spiritual transformation that Christians call *Resurrection,* a new impetus of hope defying (rather than denying) the crucifixion inherent in every death experience, individual, collective or cultural.

Since most people in Western culture spend most of their time and energy in the standard institutions of our society – family, workplace, Church, factory, educational/social/political/economic system – we find it extremely difficult to accept that the system is declining or dying. And if we do accept that demise, our first response is: rescue and save it! But it may not be possible to save it; it may not be even appropriate to do so!

The major institutions belong to an old order; they are based on a quality and type of consciousness (the mechanistic world view) that has largely outlived its usefulness. It has served us well (though some may disagree), and now we need

85

to allow it – indeed, enable it – to fade into history. The challenge of our time is to move towards the new vision; a wholistic interdisciplinary, interdependent, global ambience, demanding a whole new institutional framework, which I am suggesting is already birthing the networking orientation.

Because institutions are so powerful and so resistant to change (and death), we are dealing here with what may prove to be the most stubborn aspect of the current, global transition. And the accompanying shift in the mental sphere (the realm of perception and thought) is equally precarious; we shall explore that subject in our next chapter.

Bibliography:

Fletcher, Ronald (1988), *The Shaking of the Foundations,* London & New York: Routledge.

Lipnack, J. & Stamps, J. (1986), *The Networking Book,* Routledge and Kegan Paul.

Naisbitt, John (1982), *Megatrends: Ten New Directions Transforming our Lives,* London & Sydney: McDonald & Co.

8

From Linear to Lateral Thinking

Knowledge and fact has overwhelmed us and, in direct proportion, Wisdom has disappeared.

Sam Keen

How is change brought about? Do we begin by trying to alter attitudes and understanding, as a result of which people will modify their behaviour? Or do we begin by changing structures and ways of behaving which in turn will affect attitudes and outlook? This is a classic chicken-and-egg situation for which social scientists have no clear answer.

It is widely assumed that thought precedes action, that what we do is the consequence of how we think and perceive. Consequently, if we modify the thought and perceptual patterns, we assume we can alter behaviour and action. Behavioural psychologists have never accepted this view, and while I do not endorse their extreme mechanistic perception of the human personality, I do endorse their conviction that changed behaviour is a much more powerful means of activating growth than altered attitudes or perceptions.

I have reservations about this debate, particularly its dualistic undertones. Why does it have to be an either/or? In the wholistic paradigm of the human personality, both mental (internal) and active (external) aspects are necessary for growth and development. The question, therefore, for consideration in this chapter is: What quality of thought or perception best augments the evolution of consciousness that we deem appropriate for this age of transition?

THE LINEAR APPROACH

In the past, our thinking and perceiving tended to be predominantly *linear*. We used information for its own sake in order to solve problems. The process was conceived as being a straight line of logical, sequential progression, excluding all that was perceived to be irrelevant to the goal one wished to achieve. Much emphasis was placed on clarity, purpose, along with the skills and techniques of how to get there. It was an achievement-motivated task.

Linear (or what De Bono calls *vertical*) thought cherishes simplicity. Complexity is perceived to be irrelevant, perhaps dangerous; therefore, we ignore or bypass it. As in traditional science, the linear thought aims to discover the ultimate building blocks, which are considered to be unique, self-contained (closed) and elementary.

The underlying logic is that of cause and effect. There can only be *one* basic explanation as to why something happened and there must be *one* ultimate consequence to every line of action. At the end of the day, there can only be one correct resolution to any problem.

Obviously, we are veering towards a deterministic, rigid, stereotyped analysis. Rarely do we adhere to this literal procedure, but a great deal of our thinking and acting has been – and still is – governed by these rather simplistic, categorical and naive thought-patterns.

Meanwhile, the neatness and efficiency of the linear approach have outgrown their usefulness, and have increasingly become obstacles to progress. Unknowingly, we have adopted a new thought and perceptual model, which De Bono calls *lateral* thinking. Its features complement many of the other 'alternatives' explored in this book.

TWO THOUGHT PATTERNS

LINEAR	LATERAL
1. Selects one pathway and excludes all others. 'I know what I'm looking for.'	Generates and explores as many alternative approaches as possible. 'I

won't know what I'm looking for until I have found it.'

2. Move only when there is a clear direction; an experiment is designed to show some effect.

Move in order to generate a direction; an experiment is designed in order to provide an opportunity to change one's ideas.

3. Sequential – one step at a time.

Quantum – I can jump to the conclusion, in one or many jumps; I may have to retrace the pathway to see how I got to the solution.

4. Follows the most likely paths.

Likes to explore the less likely paths – they could be more adventuresome.

5. One has to be correct with every step.

One can learn from mistakes.

6. Categories, classifications and labels tend to be fixed.

Pigeon-holing or labelling may be useful, not for identification but as signposts to help movement.

7. Uses the negative to block off certain pathways and excludes what it perceives to be irrelevant.

The negative may be the path to breakthrough; even conflict and chance can be creative.

8. A finite process – with a definite start and finish.

Open ended; the process rather than the solution is perceived to be more important.

Lateral thinking seeks to supersede the narrow and utilitarian limits of the linear form. Laterally-minded people think big, broadly, provocatively and creatively. Problems are not obstacles for which they must find a solution, but rather challenges that will (in all probability) open up new ways of perceiving and understanding reality. For the lateral thinker, there is always something new to be learned; exploration never ends and new discoveries will never cease.

But is this realistic? We live in a practical world where we have to make pragmatic decisions. One may argue that lateral thinking is OK for armchair philosophers, but it doesn't seem very useful for negotiating the exigencies of daily life. Yet there is obviously a swing towards lateral thought patterns; there is a transition from the linear to the lateral. Why?

Like all the transitions explored in this book, we cannot offer a comprehensive rationale for the linear/lateral polarity. Undoubtedly, it is one more manifestation of the evolutionary shift we believe to be happening at the present time; something we can only verify with hindsight, perhaps in a few hundred years from now.

It is also consistent with the explosion of knowledge and information that marks our time. To cope with the quantity and complexity of new information, we have invented an external 'brain', namely *computerisation*. It is legitimate to suggest that we also need an internal 'computer' of which our capacity for lateral thinking may be the fuel or energy. Why we are developing this innate capacity at this time could be explained in terms of Darwin's 'survival of the fittest' theory, or alternatively in terms of the emerging cosmology which suggests that we live in a self-organising universe wherein every life-form 'adjusts' to the fresh demands of progress and/or evolution.

CAN THE BRAIN THINK LATERALLY?

There is a still more compelling explanation focussing on the nature of the human brain itself. At the beginning of the present century, M. Wertheimer, K. Koffka and W. Kohler pioneered the Gestalt School of human psychology. They were particularly interested in human perception, and laid the bold claims that humans do not think partially or fragmentally, but wholistically. For example, I look out of the window at a nearby house; an image registers in my brain. I can describe the image of that house, noting its various features. As far as I am concerned, I have mentally examined the house and ignored everything else in the surrounding environment.

According to Gestalt psychologists, I perceived a great deal more than just the house; I also noted in my mind the total geographical/situational context, to such a degree that if that same house was situated elsewhere my perception – in minute details – would be considerably different. In other words, *innately* I perceive in *wholes,* not in parts; my brain is tuned to perceive wholistically.

This theory received scant attention until Karl Pribram began his explorations of the holographic nature of the brain in the late 1960s and early 1970s. Pribram postulates that the human brain functions like a hologram: a three-dimensional image, when illuminated (by a laser beam) at any one point, will show up the entire image.

Pribram's initial work was on *memory storage.* How does the human brain store memories? For a number of years, neuroscientists speculated that memory was both recorded and stored in higher brain centres. Pribram decided to test a new hypothesis: memory is not encoded in any *one* centre, but distributed throughout the brain. Using intricate mathematics, he speculated that the brain functions as a *hologram,* interpreting bioelectric frequencies, not at individual centres, but throughout the brain. Information is not localised, but spread throughout in wave-like, frequency patterns along a network of fine fibres on the nerve cells. Only such a model could interpret a holographical universe.

Being equipped with holographic brains essentially means that we are capable of adjusting, accommodating and integrating vast varieties of information, even of a paradoxical nature. At a perceptual/learning level, we seem to be innately tuned for the lateral mode into which contemporary thought and perceptual patterns are projecting us. Alternatively, one could argue that it is the maturation of our wholistic brains that is bringing about the transition we describe in this chapter.

CHALLENGE FOR EDUCATION

Whatever the precise explanation, the neat, simplistic logic of yesterday seems inadequate and inappropriate for the emerging lateral vision. And this raises awkward and challenging questions for pedagogy and education. The infrastructure of the Western educational system, with the focus on achievement and competence (via public exams) – to perform effectively in a competitive, market society – is very linear in thought and in orientation. Consequently, the educational system is lagging behind considerably; a great deal of what is being taught in our schools and higher institutions of learning is of little value for this time of transition, and probably of less value for the emerging wholistic world view.

But there may be yet a more serious problem, one of developmental and even ethical significance. If the human brain, in its basic natural design is essentially holographic and wholistic; if, *by nature,* we take in reality, not in isolated fragmented sections but contextually, ie. in large chunks of experience, then our linear-based approach is not merely inappropriate, but damaging and destructive to the human personality. If education is intended to nurture the *whole* person into a more developed and enlightened being, then this must be done by reinforcing rather than by militating against our innate potentialities and abilities.

That the human brain is essentially holographic and that of its own nature it perceives laterally rather than linearly, is not an established scientific fact. It is only a theory, but as credible and as substantive as any other theory that prevails at the present time. The tendency in education to treat each discipline independently, with little or no interdisciplinary skills, is not the fruit of thorough scientific research. It is merely the logical, utilitarian consequence of a dominantly mechanistic culture, which tends to divide and fragment all life's experience into basic building blocks, where everything is treated in specialised isolation. Our educational system is largely the product of the industrial era, and *still* is largely geared to preserving and maintaining the mechanistic consciousness that belongs to a past evolutionary phase of our development as a species.

Now that we are moving (or have moved) into the information age, which among other things throws new light on the human personality (our bodies, brains, feelings, perceptions etc), we need a whole new pedagogy of education. It is inappropriate and even immoral to continue to *mechanically interfere* with the human mind when our mental capacities seem to be *non-mechanical* in their essential nature. For the information era, we need a new educational policy and fresh skills to cope with the masses of information that impinge daily upon our consciousness. The exciting challenge is that we don't have to procure those skills from *without:* increasingly, we are realizing that they are all *within.* Can we create an educational system that will activate them appropriately?

PROMISE AND THREAT

The transition from linear to lateral thought raises no small threat to our established institutions. If more and more people are encouraged to think laterally, then people will demand the space and scope to act laterally. Institutions, with the emphasis on order and organisation, do not take lightly to this prospect. It awakens fear and suspicion, the fear of 'chaos' that cannot be controlled; the suspicion that the 'powerless' (who should be kept in their place) might become 'powerful'. Lateral thinking, therefore, is likely to flourish outside rather than within the main institutions of Church or State.

Laterally-minded people thrive on creativity. They like to do things differently, and they enjoy dealing with problems in a more roundabout way. They are not inclined to rush in and stamp-out the problem before things get out of control. They trust the wholistic process, within which they perceive everything – even chaos – to have a function and a purpose. For the lateral thinker, a problem offers challenge and hope; for a linear thinker, it tends to awaken fear and a sense of threat.

The transition from the linear to the lateral – like all the transitions outlined in this book – is likely to meet with much resistance. Because our dominant thinking-mode is a linear one, we resist change and we fear the new; worst of all, our educational system powerfully endorses the linear mode, and despite all the talk about reforming the educational system, there are few signs that a lateral mode is being adopted.

Meanwhile, the transition unfolds with the majority of people locked into the linear pattern. But there are creative minorities who think differently – laterally and wholistically – and these are the catalysts of change who offer us hope for the emerging world of the new tomorrow.

Bibliography:

De Bono, Edward (1970), *Lateral Thinking: A Textbook of Creativity,* London: Ward Lock Educational Ltd.

Pribram, Karl (1971), *Languages of the Brain,* Prentice-Hall.

Wilber, Ken (Ed.) (1982), *The Holographic Principle and Other Paradoxes,* Boulder & London: New Science Library.

9

From Masculine to Feminine Authority

> *'Women do not sit nor have we ever sat at the tables where war games are drawn up, where the world's financial resources are parcelled out, where bishops are chosen or encyclicals written. Yet, we must live with the consequences.'*
>
> Jane Blewett (1989)

No issue raises more hackles today than the feminist movement. Whether it be women in politics, women's ordination, equal job opportunity, working mothers or the use of inclusive language, we are dealing with an emotive topic of passion and import. What a few years ago seemed no more than a marginalised, disgruntled minority, has become a groundswell movement, threatening to undermine much of what is precious and sacred to Western civilisation.

In this chapter, we deal with one of the more potent aspects of the transition being explored throughout this book. It is powerful, not because women – the powerless for so long – are now reclaiming their power, but because it awakens the *feminine* within all of us, and we are unsure how to handle the ensuing experience. So what do we mean by the *feminine*?

Before attempting an answer, let us try to contextualise this new development. In Part One, I spelt out the implications of the mechanistic world view, with its emphasis on parts v wholes ('divide and conquer'), manipulation, control and domination. Everything existed to be exploited and conquered, so that it could be used to benefit human beings, the masters of the created order.

In this world view, masters were *men,* and women were their chattels, who bore them children (preferably sons) to continue the battle of conquering and controlling. Culturally and historically, this is very much a development of the past two thousand years, dominating Western civilisation from the seventeenth to the twentieth century. What is important in this orientation is not so much the suppression of women (demeaning though that was) as the repression of the *feminine* in men and women alike, undermining the role of women in particular.

We are emerging from a protracted era of *patriarchy,* a cultural world view that perceives all life to emerge from the male (God), fathering that robust and energetic individual who fought the alien forces and thus made the planet habitable for human beings. For this gregarious male, everything is perceived to be threatening, although inferior and capable of being conquered and controlled. There emerges the rudimentary notion of a hierarchy validated by the supreme God, under whose guidance everything is to be managed and manipulated in a rational, controlled, structured world order.

Feeling, imagination, intuition and creativity are all held to be suspect; they are not easily managed or controlled, and they militate against the male passion for absolute power. Spirituality, too, is suspect; it has connotations of weakness and dependency, and these cannot be entertained since they subvert the will to power.

This is a caricature of the *masculine,* stated, perhaps, in its most extreme form; not an overstatement, however, in a world that tends to exterminate the useless, decry the gentle and sensitive, and exploit the universe for selfish gain. Patriarchy (or masculine consciousness) is alive and well, reigning so powerfully within Church and State alike that nobody dared to question its absolute autonomy until recent times. But with so many chinks in the armoury, civilisation could no longer turn a blind eye to its inherent destructability.

Only a few years ago, it sounded so good to be told that we humans had made enormous progress in conquering alien forces, whether personal issues of disease and illness, or global concerns of poverty and scientific ignorance. But have we made 'enormous progress', and what price have we paid for this so-called 'progress'? We have extended the human lifespan, yet invented a whole new set of 'civilised' diseases such as coronary ailments, cancers and stress-related illnesses. We have made enormous strides in the development of technology, but in the process of doing so we have turned Planet Earth into an ecological cess-pool. We have highlighted the plight of the impoverished majority of Earth's people, but deviously we have continued to exploit the South to feed a power-hungry, extortionist North. Our so-called progress has brought some relief, but ironically an enormous amount of pain and misery.

It is at this precarious juncture that the *feminine* begins to unfold. Perhaps once again we are experiencing something of a death/resurrection paradigm. From the depth of destruction and despair arises the unexpected seed of hope; from the chaos emerges creativity!

FEMININE CONSCIOUSNESS

In its cultural and historical meaning, the *feminine* is to be understood as the complementary (not the opposite) value to the *masculine*. At all times our culture needs *both,* but there are historical epochs when one is more needed than the other. While the *masculine* articulates a compulsive need to dominate and control, the feminine extols the inner freedom of 'let be' and 'let go'. The feminine has no urge to control because it senses (from the heart) that all life-forms unfold according to their own inherent dynamism. From the feminine perspective, *waiting, listening* and respectfully *allowing* life to unfold are the most desirable qualities.

And this is no mere passivity! Rather, it is a highly-developed sensitivity, a deep feeling for the pain and ecstasy that marks every new becoming, whether it be the continuous birth of new cells in the human body or the evolutionary shifts that happen every 50,000 years or so. The feminine is a power of the *heart:* the masculine is focussed in the head. The former thrives on feeling, the latter on cerebral thought.

Emerging as we are from a protracted era of masculine consciousness, the pendulum is swinging very much to the other side. The energies must be balanced because the universe needs both sets of qualities. Moreover, the transition taking place, like all major evolutionary shifts, defies rational explanation. The masculine mind-set cannot grasp, comprehend or 'control' what's going on. The feminine outlook is what is most urgently needed at this time. The feminine can live with the chaos of change; it does not suffer from the male obsession for law and order. Indeed, it believes that the chaos can be life-giving and highly creative.

FEATURES OF THE FEMININE

Madonna Kolbenschlag (speaking at a women's conference at Washington DC, 9-13 October 1986) identified four features which characterise the feminist consciousness: *passion, imagination, resistance* and *solidarity*. These qualities merit some further elucidation.

1. **Passion:** The word comes from the Latin *passio* and the Greek *pathos,* meaning suffering or intense feeling. In early Christian times, and frequently since then, *apatheia* was considered to be a prerequisite for a mature spiritual life. The ideal holy person should not be passionately involved in life; (s)he should assume a sense of aloofness, dismissing the concerns of the world as illusive and transitory. Because women are essentially creatures of feeling and innately passionate, they were considered to be sources of temptation for men; consequently, females were to be shunned and avoided by those seriously committed to spiritual growth. This perverse spirituality still prevails, albeit in a mitigated form – especially in some of the main religious traditions of both East and West.

The emerging feminine consciousness, struggling with the *apatheia* of the past, strives to reassert the wholesomeness of the body, the sacredness of the Earth and the power of creativity, especially in sexuality and fertility. It is passionately committed to the unfolding of human and earthly potentiality, with the pain, suffering and death (on the one hand), and the ecstasy and rebirth (on the other) that are involved in this process.

It strives above all to restore *emotion* and *feeling* to their lawful place, reminding us that we cannot be people of heart in a heartless world unless and until we can share the anger, rage and pain, along with the *eros*, ecstasy and joy that characterise our world. The feminine refuses to subvert feelings, even if they are too painful to endure. The masculine fear of the inner (and outer) chaos is precisely where the feminine seeks renewed growth and vitality.

While the masculine consciousness strives to move forward, by denial and repression of 'messy feelings', by categorising and compartmentalising human experience, by controlling and organising social and ecological reality, the feminine adopts a more receptive and contemplative stance, exposing the self to the unfolding experience of life in all its untidiness and creativity as it awaits the inherent outcome of what it believes to be an essentially (pro)creative world. While the product at the end of the line preoccupies the *masculine observer,* it is the unfolding and mysterious process that fascinates the *feminine participant.*

2. **Imagination:** To think logically, reasonably and rationally is the target of our male-dominated culture. We feel quite uncomfortable with, if not threatened by, the poet, the dreamer, the person strongly endowed with intuition and imagination. Our brains are somewhat twisted and distorted by an educational system that exaggerates the left hemisphere of rationality and underplays the right sphere of intuition and creativity.

Since the feminine is essentially an energy of the heart rather than the head, it tends to articulate its vision and perception in a different mode. According to Regina Bechtle (1988 p.53) 'Feminist spirituality draws on the power of imagination to develop symbols which mirror alternative views of reality.' This is a loaded statement. It captures something of the power inherent in the feminine vision; it suggests the ability to comprehend in depth – at a symbolic level, where life is considered in its deeper, wholistic sense, rather than at the superficial, external level which preoccupies our masculine mode of consciousness.

Bechtle also suggests that 'dreaming alternatives' is peculiar to the feminine consciousness. Perhaps this is the very reason why woman-power has long been perceived as a threat to the dominantly male culture and, consequently, subverted when and where possible. The feminine is never at ease with the status quo, particularly when the dominant patriarchal culture denies space for creativity, exploration and imagination. Confronted with stalemate and a conformity imposed from on high, the feminine rebels in favour of creating alternatives, breaking out of impasses and finding novel and unexpected solutions to human and cultural problems.

By adopting this strategy, the feminine engenders *hope*, particularly for the poor, the oppressed and the marginalised, who feel either deprived or patronised in patriarchal societies. Dreaming the alternatives that offer hope is quite a subversive activity. Usually it implies much more than changing power structures; instead it sets out to create *alternative* models. The women's movement is a typical example of this orientation, and the ordination to the bishopric of Barbara Harris in 1989 illustrates the option to create the alternative reality without waiting for the mainstream culture to approve of this new development.

Networking (explored in Chapter Seven) very often veers in this direction. Instead of looking to the mainstream institutions for support or approval, the networkers sense a whole new way of doing things, and press ahead to realize their vision. It is not a conscious choice to flaunt or undermine an existing system; it arises from a profound sense (difficult to put into words) that the mainstream institutions no longer serve people's deepest needs. A degree of confrontation is inevitable, and this leads to my third consideration of the feminine approach.

3. **Resistance:** Herbert Marcuse once said that for an institution to be successful, it must make unthinkable the possibility of alternatives. In other words, institutions of their nature are self-perpetuating, and this being the case, they oppose any developments that form a threat to their autonomy. The feminine resistance, therefore, is an attempt to place people before systems, and to continually remind the system that people are more important than things. The

resistance becomes a struggle for justice, especially on behalf of the poor and marginalised.

The encounter with suffering is central to this undertaking. The masculine consciousness considers pain, suffering and death as alien forces to be conquered and controlled; when this is not possible, we numb people against their impact. Western society has invented a complex repertoire of death-denying strategies, ranging from projected violence on film and television to escapist pleasure often focused on sex or alcohol, to subverted feelings by the use of a wide range of legal and illegal drugs, to macho competition as exemplified in many male-dominated sports. Because our society is loath to look honestly and straight in the face of human suffering, then we often (unconsciously) impose suffering on innocent people. Our society is engulfed in a death-ridden culture (from sadistic pleasure on the one hand, to warfare on the other), largely because we are out of tune with our *feelings* about death, pain and suffering.

The feminine consciousness strives to acknowledge pain and suffering for what they really are: not for the sake of tolerating them, but outgrowing them in an appropriate process of encounter and growth. By denying our pain, we give it power over us. By acknowledging it, we can more readily perceive its origins (often in sinful, 'male' structures), and set out to rectify the injustices that make pain and suffering intolerable and meaningless. It is by no accident that when Jesus was dying on the Hill of Calvary, he was accompanied mainly by women; virtually all the menfolk had fled in fear. And when he read the resurrection story (the hope-story) of the first Easter morn, those who had no trouble in believing and sharing in the hope were those same *women* who shared the suffering to the end, and not the menfolk who thought the women were talking mere rubbish (cf. Lk.24:11).

The struggle and resistance epitomised in the feminine consciousness exhibits a rare profundity, touching some of the deepest feelings and aspirations of human and earthly life. Without this ability to grapple with the injustice which causes so much meaningless suffering in our world, our lives and our culture will be all the poorer.

4. Solidarity: Feminism seeks a whole new approach to the exercise of power. It seeks power that is shared rather than imposed from on high. Its primary goal is not the demolition of old power structures, but rather the recreation of human communion, where power becomes the gift we use to empower each other.

This is the networking image, characterised by connections, relatedness and the sharing of resources. It is power emanating from the centre and shared equally by all. It is a power to be given away, precisely to empower those who feel alienated and excluded.

These are noble aspirations, which few people will quibble about. Where differences of opinion will arise is on the 'how'. The masculine consciousness is happy to empower as long as *it* is doing the empowering. The idea that the rich could be empowered by the poor, the healthy by the sick, men by women, is so preposterous as to be considered ridiculous. But this is the *feminine* challenge, one of the most provocative and creative at the present time.

Feminist power also suggests a new style of management. It is no longer the boss at the top, nor the manager (cum management-team) who runs the show. One is not suggesting that everybody does everything, which, in practice, is a prescription for anarchy. In feminist terms, chaos may be creative; therefore, be open to what may evolve from a whole new way of doing things. As long as we accompany each other in trust and solidarity, we can handle the outcome; let's be open to originality and innovation!

It is this daring, courageous and risky attitude that characterises the feminine sense of solidarity, which strives to reclaim human community in its various and possible forms. It is not an 'opposite' to the masculine, hierarchical approach; it is a complementary and equally valid (although, today, largely unknown) way of operating. And it would seem to be eminently appropriate to that stage of evolutionary growth that characterises our time.

TWO MODELS OF AUTHORITY

MASCULINE	FEMININE
1. Control and domination.	Stewardship and dialogue.
2. Operate from the thinking centre (the head).	Feel with the heart.
3. Be logical and rational.	Use your imagination.
4. Aggression: conquer and subdue the earth.	Receptivity and gentleness: why ravage the womb that nurtures us?
5. Suppress feelings.	Acknowledge feelings.
6. Maintain a stiff upper-lip and don't cry.	Trust your feelings.
7. We believe only what we can verify and prove.	'Blessed are those who have not seen and yet believe.'
8. Distinction and differences are important.	All people are equal.

COMPLEMENTARY MODES

The reflections in this chapter focus on a transition from the dominant male-power image (top-down), to the emerging female-enabling image (from the centre out). Masculine authority tends to be focused largely, if not exclusively, on the 'boss' at the top of the hierarchical ladder; feminine power is essentially *inclusive* of everybody, with the focus on power equally shared.

Masculine power tends to operate in *isolation,* above and beyond those being governed, percolating downwards through a series of layers, to the rank and file. Feminine power is about new forms of *togetherness* (participation), sharing all our resources cooperatively, and thus empowering those who otherwise feel excluded and alienated.

Masculine power is validated by the history, culture and spirituality of the recent past. Feminine power is a new phenomenon for which there are few if any prescriptive guidelines. As one American feminist states: 'The paths are not marked for us because they have not yet been walked.'

Masculine power is not just about men ruling women, nor is feminine power the opposite of this. In today's world, many women operate the masculine system even more effectively than men, and an increasing number of men are resonating with, and endorsing, the emerging feminine consciousness. Gender is not the issue at stake; our concern is about two modes of responding which we characterise as *masculine* and *feminine.*

And yet these reflections have deep personal implications. Contrary to some current liberal ideas, we assert that by nature we are essentially *male* or *female,* and these are not mere stereotypes imposed by society. Whether we are male or female, we each possess a feminine and masculine dimension. At times, one may be stronger than the other, and different circumstances in life will elicit one disposition rather than the other. The ideal is not so much one of balancing both as being sensitive to the fact that both are always active to varying degrees; the sensitivity necessary for this awareness is itself a feminine trait.

What we are experiencing at the present time is that issues of a global/cultural nature, such as the emerging feminine consciousness, are having profound effects on individual, personal growth. For so long we have thought and acted in terms of *we* affecting (and changing) the world out there, as characteristic of the masculine mode. Now we are beginning to understand ourselves anew in the light of the world around us, and its potential to effect change in our lives, even at a profoundly personal level.

Many things are being turned upside down. As long as we remember that it is a chaos that can be immensely creative, then our exposure to its impact won't destroy us. In fact, we may find ourselves, surprisingly, born anew!

Bibliography:

Bechtle, Regina (1988), 'Reclaiming the truth of Women's Lives: Women and Spirituality', *The Way,* Vol.28, pp.50-59.

Ferguson, Marilyn (1982), *The Aquarian Conspiracy: Personal and Social Transformation in the 1980s,* Routledge and Kegan Paul.

King, Ursula (1989), *Women and Spirituality: Voices of Protest and Promise,* London: Macmillan.

Morgan, Robin (1982), *The Anatomy of Freedom: Feminism, Physics and Global Politics,* New York: Anchor Press/Doubleday.

10

From Production to Process Marketing

It is the pattern that is of interest, not the state of any particular node.

Paul C.W. Davies

In the days before marketing became a 'science', firms used to believe that their products would carry on selling virtually forever. This belief rested on the assumption that (a) the consumer would continue to buy the same product over a long period of time, and (b) that no competitor entered the market with a better version of the same product.

Strange though it may seem to the modern reader, this static, highly predictable trend dominated the industrial world up to and including the 1960s. With the onset of breakdown in the mechanistic world view, the closed, linear marketing model also began to crumble.

The traditional consumer was a person whose needs were mechanistically defined by the prevailing culture. Society was highly structured; expectations clearly understood, and human behaviour followed broadly and widely accepted patterns. Even if different brands of coffee came on the market, you stuck to the familiar; you did not risk changing to something new. Experimentation in taste or fashion was largely unknown and certainly not approved. A type of mass culture prevailed, and practically everybody assumed it was natural and normal.

The factory was the site of production, and the employees operated the plant to produce the goods. The workers rarely thought of themselves as producers in any way other than in a mechanical sense. Work was significant for earning a wage that

106

enabled one to do more productive things, such as establish a home, rear a family and enjoy oneself, outside the context of work.

CHANGING ATTITUDES

Already in the 1970s the attitude to the workplace was changing, or, perhaps it was merely a case of bringing out into the open the underlying grudges that could never be aired in what was essentially a closed system. In the mid-1970s an article in the London *Times* began with these words:

> 'Dante, when composing his vision of Hell, might well have included the mindless, repetitive boredom of working on a factory assembly line. It destroys initiative and rots brains; yet millions of British workers are committed to it for most of their lives.'

Strangely, there was no reaction to this statement, either positively or negatively. Perhaps the statement was reflecting accurately something of the transition that was beginning to take place. Consumers had become more enterprising. The 1960s had awoken a sense of creativity whereby people sought novelty, variety and excitement. A staid, monotonous market no longer satisfied the consumer, increasingly avid for new goods. Some firms went to the wall or were threatened with closure. Those who survived had to make fast and radical adjustments.

Trade unions assumed a new importance. Jobs were under threat, and managers, in their urgency to salvage an enterprise, often treated the workforce with contempt and with blatant disregard. Strikes became rampant and prolonged, often achieving little beyond extending the existence of a beleagured institution for a few more years. Unemployment and redundancies became daily issues, throwing large numbers of people into personal confusion and social disarray. Chaos reigned in the market place.

The transition in the industrial/marketing sphere had a double impetus. People demanded novelty and variety, while the market place itself, at many different levels – was archaic and unsuited to the modern, technological world. Therefore there was a consumer challenge from without and a massive restructuring necessitated from within. The problem became greatly exacerbated by the fact that the internal reform did not – perhaps could not – keep pace with the demands from outside. In many cases, trade unions tried to block and jeopardise the transition; in the majority of cases the unions were the losers, even to the extent of usurping their own credibility in most European countries.

Along with an enlightened and more articulate consumer, the market had (and still has) to cope with a rapidly expanding technological world. Although computerisation came into its own in the 1960s, it had only a limited impact on the industrial sphere prior to the 1970s. Now a machine could do in one day what formerly twenty workers could only do in one week. Obviously, the workers lost out and were made redundant.

Many institutions in our society agonise over the supremacy of the machine, particularly its power to undermine the human right to work. Although trade unionists readily acknowledge the need for, and efficiency of, mechanisation and computerisation, they have battled long and hard to 'save jobs', as if this was the ultimate criterion of a successful business. Herein is one of the great dilemmas of the transition we explore in this chapter.

THE PARADOX OF UNEMPLOYMENT

Work in Western societies defines our status and significance. It is the medium through which we express our sense of being useful and productive. It provides for many people a social and psychological context, in the absence of which their lives literally fall to pieces. Consequently, unemployment is considered to be one of the supreme evils of our time, and full employment is the goal which every government sets among its priorities.

The work ethic underpining these considerations is flawed with contradictions. Firstly, the human desire (and right) to work is a great deal more than doing a job that earns a wage.

Work is a dimension of human creativity, the need to activate oneself and one's talents in realizing one's inner potential and thus to feel useful by contributing to the unfolding of universal life. People need to be affirmed for their work in more ways than merely financial remuneration. In actual fact, most adults do not earn money for their work; they operate in what is known as the *informal* economy.

A corollary to this observation is that human beings – unconsciously for the greater part – have been trying to humanise work for quite a long time. Externally and superficially, we can argue that the Industrial Revolution set out to make work and productivity more efficient. But the deeper and more pervasive motivation was to strip work of its pain and drudgery so that people could have time and energy for more creative pursuits.

Deep within the mythic vision of the Industrial Revolution is an aspiration for what we now call the age of leisure. I wish to suggest that this has been, and still is, the ultimate goal of industrialisation. Consequently, we continue to mechanise 'jobs' so that we can liberate ourselves, not *from* work, but *for* creativity. Unemployment is not the great curse we perceive it to be; in a subtle, but very real sense, we have brought this mixed blessing upon ourselves.

Governments that continue to promise full employment are deluding the people for the sake of political expediency. Even if full employment could be realized, it may prove to be highly inappropriate. We are moving beyond the 'jobs-for-money' stage of our evolution. It is inappropriate and psychologically crippling to seek growth and affirmation in the 'physical' (materialistic) context of a 'job' and 'money', when essentially we are being invited to move into a new 'psychic' age (see Chapter 12).

I don't believe there is anything naive, unreal or superficial about these ideas. They seem to be a logical and coherent outcome of the historical, cultural and technological developments of the past few hundred years. As ideas they have reached the stage of maturity and are demanding profound cultural and structural changes. Not least among these is the provision of a living wage for each person, whether employed or unemployed; that is an issue many governments will have to confront, possibly before the end of the present century.

We are now in a position to describe more clearly what we mean by the title of this chapter. The old consciousness, which still dominates our Western thought patterns, is one of *production*. We attribute major importance to the *object* we produce at the end of the production line. Our sense of achievement, satisfaction and fulfilment is wrapped up in this outcome.

Yet many people do not see any great beauty or elegance in the object of their production; frequently these days they don't even see it. And they are not particularly concerned as long as it means *hard cash* in their hand at the end of the week.

By identifying so closely with the *objects* we produce we have, in many cases, turned ourselves into mechanised, objectified robots, deprived of feeling and imagination. The traditional workplace may have provided 'a secure job', but in most cases it was, humanly and spiritually, a stultifying place to work in. It suited the masculine consciousness of the time – therefore, it tended to be *men* who *worked* – but it is grossly inappropriate for the emerging world we experience today.

PROCESS AND MOVEMENT

I am suggesting the transition is towards *process,* a fashionable, contemporary word with a variety of meanings. In the present context, *process* refers to what's going on, within and among the people, the factory, the nation, the world, that provides the wider context within which we produce one or other object (see table).

A practical example is that of the traditional educational system which often measured success by the number of A levels attained at the end of the 'production line'. The A levels served as an indication of how *useful* and *successful* the person would be in the *productive* economy. In the *process* context, the focus is not on the A levels attained at the *end,* but on all that goes on in that person's life *during* his or her years at school; particular importance would be attributed to the development of friendships, skills attained, growth in maturity, improved self-image and a growing identity as a citizen of

110

Planet Earth. In this context, the usefulness to society is understood to arise from inner conviction and vision, rather than focussing on external achievement.

TWO APPROACHES TO MARKETING

PRODUCTION	PROCESS
1. Mechanical and structured.	Fluid, flexible and highly adaptable.
2. The end product is all-important.	What is really important is the interaction taking place in the production process.
3. People tend to become cogs in the machine.	People own the process and are not owned by it.
4. The outcome must be utilitarian, functional and quantifiable.	The outcome is determined by the quality of ongoing interaction rather than the quantity of goods produced.
5. Predictable: we know where we stand with the process.	Open-ended, fluid, open to surprise and creativity.
6. People are trained once and for ever; skills are passed on from longstanding members to initiates.	Retraining is essential for everybody; at all times, members must be open to acquiring new skills.
7. Hierarchical leadership is crucial.	Even if hierarchical leadership prevails, delegation and subsidiarity of function is central to the realization of everybody's potential.

8. Change is resisted because it is perceived to be disruptive and dangerous.	People are enthusiastic about change; it fosters growth and enhances the flexibility of the interaction.
9. The cultural horizon is on the here-and-now and focused on the plant/enterprise itself.	The horizon stretches far beyond the project/enterprise, often adopting a global ambience.

Process is very much about *movement.* It seeks to establish that we are outgrowing our production mentality and aspiring to something much more generic and wholistic. We think in terms of producing in cooperation with others, rejoicing in the mutual enrichment of diverse gifts and talents; hence the rise of cooperatives in the past few decades. We seek to break down the traditional dividing lines between management and workers, a process that already has been activated in many parts of the world with varying degrees of success. In not a few cases today, workers and management jointly run projects and share profits equally.

And we take on board wide ecological and political considerations. Various attempts have been made to trade not just for profit but for a more suitable distribution of goods. Environmentally, we are much more educated about, and sensitive towards, questions of industrial pollution. Within workplaces, safety and health standards have improved considerably.

MANIFESTATIONS OF TRANSITION

The notion of process or movement is nowhere more apparent than in the sense of innovation that permeates the commercial world of today. Public libraries abound with books on entrepreneurial skills, setting up one's own business, innovative management, flexible work arrangements, etc. What was once a stable, static, conventional and clearly-defined realm of life is now a buzz-world of fresh ideas, bold initiatives and experimental projects.

112

In the industrial and commercial spheres, there are two other developments of a process flavour: communication of information and personnel management. Since many enterprises today – even very small ones – belong to worldwide networks, the communication and processing of information has become vitally important. And with the introduction of computerisation, all information concerning a plant or project is often available to *all* the workers. The process of communicating information has assumed central importance in today's commercial world.

Rationalisation and mechanisation have had some positive fringe benefits for workers. Despite the newly acquired power and status of the machine, people are perceived to be more important than ever. In fact, the various attempts to consult and integrate people into an enterprise owe some credit to the tedious and persevering work of trade union leaders. Many projects now employ personnel managers, not merely to provide a platform for airing grievances, but on the assumption that the success of an enterprise largely depends on the participation of all involved in it. Increasingly, the worker is considered to be not an outside observer, but a full participant in a joint project.

Finally, the process taking place within the economic and industrial sphere is, as already noted, symptomatic of the wider global shifts from the closed, static unit to the open and creative arena. We live in a very creative age, with expanding horizons and aspirations towards higher and more spiritual ways of being. None of us wants to be a mere cog in a machine, and for an increasing number of people, not even wage incentives attract them to certain jobs. Life is bigger and broader than the job one does or the money one earns.

The transition from production to process marketing is well under way in the commercial field, although motivated still by the greed and gain focused mainly on multinational companies. At least the commercial world is acknowledging the transition and striving to respond. Most governments, however, fail to comprehend the reality; they affirm anything that smacks of success in monetary and commercial terms. They have not grasped the deeper, underlying message. They have not understood the historical and cultural context that makes process rather than production a necessity for our time.

As with most other transitions outlined in this book, there is a dire need for enlightenment and education. Perhaps the realities we describe are not yet sufficiently developed to elicit the recognition they deserve. It may even be unreal to expect such recognition from on high. The alternative consciousness arises from the grassroots, and continues to grow until it assumes the leading role of a new industrial paradigm. And that may happen sooner than we expect, since the seeds are already fermenting in the creative possibilities reviewed in this chapter.

Bibliography:

Foster, Richard N (1987), *Innovation: The Attacker's Advantage,* Pan Books.

Douglas, G., Kemp, P. & Cook, J. (Eds.) (1978), *Systematic New Product Development,* London: Associated Business Programmes.

Robertson, James (1986), *Future Work,* London: Gower.

11

From Church to Kingdom Theology

If the Church spent the last millenium in the legitimation of the established order, it is now gathering its forces in order to be an agent of change and a historical force for the humanisation of the world.

Leonardo Boff

Theology is essentially a Christian concept, derived from the Greek combination of *theos,* meaning God, and *logos,* meaning word. For many centuries, theology was considered to be the queen of the sciences, communicating God's word to humankind and interpreting the meaning of God's message for human life.

Theology was also considered to be a superior science, because it took as its subject matter God's own revealed truth. It claimed to have access to *pure* truth, and consequently set itself in opposition to all earthly learning, of which philosophy was considered to be the supreme form.

This is yet another example of dualistic thinking that has bedevilled all world religions and Christianity itself from earliest times. It also subscribes to the ideal of the 'objective observer', a concept that becomes quite extreme in Reformation times, when the text of the Christian scriptures was considered to be God's own word to humanity (as if human agencies were mere robots in its composition and compilation), a stance adopted by Muslims towards the Koran and, in varying degrees, by most Eastern religions to their sacred writings.

CHURCH AND THEOLOGY

Throughout the Middle Ages, theology had the final say in all matters relating to our understanding of the world and earthly life. Theology had a monopoly of truth. Since the Christian Church considered itself the only valid interpreter of divine truth, it was the Church rather than theologians that owned the monopoly. Hence, the (in)famous slogan: 'Outside the Church, there's no salvation.'

This statement is often associated explicitly with Catholicism. Certainly in the twentieth century, up to about 1960, when other Christian churches were becoming ecumenically-minded, Catholicism adopted a rigidly, exclusive monopoly of 'the fullness of truth'. But this is not just a Catholic problem. To this day, all the Christian churches share the belief that Christianity has an unique and favoured claim to 'revealed' truth, above and beyond the other world religions. And the defender of this unique truth is the *Church* (or churches) under its divinely-inspired leadership.

There is a sense, therefore, in which *theology* and *Church* have been, and in large measure still are, synonymous. It is assumed that theologians belong to the family of one or other church, that they explore deeper truth on behalf of the people that comprise the church, that their explorations enrich and enhance the life of the church, and that they (theologians) are faithful and answerable to the leadership of the church.

In this scenario, theology is all too often forced into a position of justifying the ecclesiastical status quo, an outcome all too familiar in Roman Catholicism. Theologians are expected to base their reflections on the Christian scriptures, not on sacred texts of other religions; they must not question nor undermine the church's official teaching, handed down in tradition eg. the sacramental system. They must not dabble in political concerns, nor in any mundane, secular issues that would undermine the spiritual purity of their work. And above all, they must accept the Church's supreme teaching authority in matters of faith and morals.

The Church, therefore, becomes the ultimate guardian and arbiter of truth. And in this case, we mean the leadership of the official, ecclesiastical institution. This image of Church is diminishing, declining, dying. In Catholicism it was officially rejected in the early 1960s in favour of a new understanding – the original Biblical meaning – consisting of *all* God's people; the Church *is* the people of God. In recent years that broadened understanding has been retracted, almost disowned, by official Church leadership.

In Europe and the USA, the church(es) continues to lose credibility:

i) Its numbers continue to decline with less than fifty per cent going to church at Christmas and Easter, and less than twenty per cent for the remainder of the year.
ii) Its influence on political, social and scientific developments is minimal; no serious thinker today pays too much attention to Church teachings.
iii) Increasing numbers of disillusioned 'believers' seek a revitalised Church in sects, cults and in a vast range of alternative spiritual movements.

The Church therefore, as a focal point for theological discourse, is a reality of the past. It belongs to the scientific paradigm where the institutional Church tried to keep balance and order within all its parts, including its theologians. Theology was a tool of the Church, an instrument of its own self-perpetuating myth. It worked well while the Church was, spiritually and sociologically, considered to be the ultimate guardian of truth. That is no longer the case, and from the ensuing chaos a whole new image of Church – and a new theological agenda – is beginning to unfold.

GOD'S NEW REIGN OF TRANSFORMATION

An interesting feature of the transition being explored in this book – possibly a feature of all major transitions – is an attempted return to original myths, to the water which is purest at the source. In the gospel teaching of Jesus, very little is said about *Church*. The Gospels focus strongly on a reality called the *Kingdom of God*. Jesus had a great deal to say about this Kingdom, and it became the context for much of his preaching and healing miracles. In the past twenty years, theological reflection has taken on a strong Kingdom orientation.

There are no obvious parallels in the other major religions. Jesus's use of the concept, however, is so global and eclectic in its ambience it is capable of incorporating rather than excluding much of what the other religions aspire towards. In the Gospels, the *Kingdom* may be described as: *A new reign of godliness brought about by divine intervention, supremely embodied in the life and ministry of Jesus, but not to be identified exclusively with Christians.* It is not confined to any particular place or human realm, nor to any one historical epoch (cf. Matt.11:11, 13:47ff; Lk.6:20, 17:20-21), not even to the present earthly order (although it includes this). Neither does it belong to human beings to control or manipulate, although humans share intimately in its existence and are invited to foster its growth and development.

The Kingdom that Jesus proclaimed is essentially about *transformation:* a new world order characterised by creative relationships of justice, love and peace. Some theologians, eg. Thomas Sheehan (1986), go so far as to suggest that the transformation in question marks the end of religion: no longer do we need religion as a means of negotiating the relationship between God 'above' and humanity here below. God in Jesus has irrevocably entered our history, turned its power structures upside down by declaring the powerless and marginalised blessed, and by dissolving himself into human and earthly history particularly in his death and resurrection. The challenge for us is to accept full responsibility for the process of transformation, initiated in and through Jesus, and commit ourselves to its unfolding by building up a world order marked by right relationships of justice, love and peace.

In biblical Christianity – particularly in the writings of St Paul – the Church is intended to be the primary activator of the Kingdom vision, and in its early days it seems to have adopted this role. St Paul himself had no small hassle with the other apostles in trying to espouse a 'global' agenda for the early Church. And at local level, the Church became the fellowship for gathering the people into a communion of mutual enrichment, where diverse gifts were acknowledged and affirmed.

In the early Church, there seems to have been little regimentation or dogmatism until the fourth or fifth centuries, when the Church began to develop its Christology (theology of Christ), and use it to dampen and denounce all others who were grappling with the significance of the Christ figure. In this very process, the Church began to lose sight of its primary agenda. Jesus did not proclaim himself – he proclaimed the Kingdom; he gave his life for the sake of the dream, but the early Church retrieved the life of Jesus not for the sake of the dream (ie. the Kingdom), but to establish its own power and credibility. And that is the great 'sin' that undermines the Church's credibility today.

In theological terms, the Church is intended to be both herald and servant of the Kingdom. Historically, the church has subverted the cause of the Kingdom and, by doing so, has turned itself into a type of self-glorifying idol, often precipitating its own downfall (cf. Boff, 1985). Despite all the rhetoric, debates, councils and assemblies, the Church in the Northern hemisphere continues to decline and its credibility continues to wane.

SOME NEW ORIENTATIONS

Meanwhile, a new theological vision begins to unfold. It is a Kingdom-based theology, chiefly in the sense that it breaks out of traditional spiritual and ecclesiastical moulds. Perhaps its most radical feature is that it takes its agenda, not from the Church (not even from the scriptures), but from the world. It seeks to listen to what the creative Spirit is doing in the midst of creation and in the lives of *all* peoples. It is alert to the *new* and to the awakening dream for the *future*.

Among such developments, perhaps the most outstanding is that of *liberation theology*, born out of the experience of struggle and oppression in the Latin American subcontinent. And the broadening horizon here is in the bridge-building between spirituality and the political (dis)order. This is a powerfully transformative situation because the political alliance is with a force (namely, Marxism) which traditionally has been labelled oppressive and dehumanising.

Another recent upsurge, with a distinctive Kingdom

119

orientation, is that of *feminist* theology. The broadening horizon here is one of including women and the feminine in what has been a very lopsided, male-dominated faith, a feature still prevailing in most of the major world religions. It is also a declaration that in God's new reign there are no racial, social or sexual distinctions; all people are equally cherished.

A third example is the theology of *multi-faith dialogue,* which invites the Christian churches to consider each religion to be an equally valid *human* attempt to grapple with the meaning of life. This may well prove to be the most difficult transition for Christianity; it would mean shedding the exclusivity which has been the basis of its power as a world force in the past.

A fourth and final example is what many people now call *creation-centred spirituality* (cf. Fox 1984). This may be described as the faith that arises from an appreciation of nature and the sacredness of our earthly existence. It seeks to salvage the Kingdom vision from ecclesiastical enclaves, cut off from *real* people in a *real* world. In a planet threatened by so many forms of pollution and desecration, this is one of the most timely theological developments of our age.

The transition I outline in this chapter is one that few people are in tune with. Those still committed to formal religious beliefs are so wrapped up in the narrow institutional vision of one or other religious or denominational system, that they are blinkered against the wider 'truth' I outline in these pages. And those who have abandoned the Church(es) – the majority of Europeans – although in many cases living out of a Kingdom-based value system, want to have nothing to do with religion, because they falsely perceive all religion to be 'churchy'. It will take some time, therefore, to clarify (and inform people) of what is involved in this theological transition from a focus on Church to a commitment to the kingdom. The two-column resumé in the following table identifies the main elements underpinning the respective orientations.

TWO THEOLOGICAL PERSPECTIVES

CHURCH	KINGDOM
1. Concerned largely with Church activities, religious behaviour and spiritual matters.	Concerned with the whole of life, especially the human realm.
2. Places Church administration and strategies above the pursuit of justice, mercy and truth.	Seek first the Kingdom of God and the justice brought about by right relationships at all levels of life.
3. Concerned about getting people into the Church.	Concerned about getting the Church into the world.
4. Preoccupied with the state of body and soul, principally the latter.	Concerned with the healing and health of the whole person – and the whole planet.
5. Outreach to the lapsed.	Outreach to people who can effect change for a more just and equitable society.
6. Ministry tends to be centred around sacramental life.	Ministry seeks to establish the human and earthly conditions to enhance God's new reign of justice, love and peace.
7. Regards the baptised as the new people of God.	Regards all – baptised or not, Christian or not – as the new people of God.
8. Hierarchical leaderships are considered to be important.	Everybody is important, particularly the poor, marginalised and

	powerless.
9. Feels threatened by variety of ideas and diversity of religious practice.	Welcomes diversity and rejoices in its enriching potential.
10. Worries that the world might change the Church.	Welcomes the world as the arena where God writes the agenda for the Church.

WHITER INSTITUTIONAL CHRISTIANITY?

This transition involves a great deal more than the Church(es) going global. It is difficult to envisage the institutional Church as it stands taking the risk of such a move. To become more Kingdom-centred would mean letting go of many or all of the institutional props and perks that are deemed indispensable, such as hierarchical structures, a dominant male priesthood, a sacramental system. In fact, the institutional Church cannot imagine itself without these realities, and what it dreads most of all is the ensuing disorder and chaos if and when it chooses to let go of its securities. That such chaos could be creative is virtually inconceivable, although the Christian Bible itself, especially the Old Testament, provides abundant examples of the potential creativity of chaos.

If this transition is to take place – and already the omens are fairly significant – one fears to think that it will be rather messy and chaotic. From the Church's perspective, it is not the untidiness of trying to make it across that is likely to create problems; in large measure the Church, like most major institutions, is able to 'control' that phenomenon. It is much more difficult to 'manage' the chaos and confusion that inevitably follow when we deny death to the bitter end.

For those unfamiliar with the evolutionary perspective of history, the growth of Christianity, covering some two thousand years, seems a very long time; in fact, it is extremely brief. For most of that time, Christianity was an European religion; it has become global only in the past two hundred years, with a great deal of its power still locked into European institutionalism or Western imperialism. The cultural transition facing Christianity today – and indeed all the major religions – is a new phenomenon; the church(es) has not been through this experience before.

So far, the churches are not doing well. They are, in fact, following the same pattern as all the major institutions of Western civilisation, desperately trying to hold on to the mechanistic power paradigm. If we are on the brink of a new evolutionary threshold, not even the churches will survive in the old mould; they, too, will fade into oblivion. And the Kingdom – if it is to survive, and I for one, believe it will – will thrive outside rather than within the institutional churches.

The Church, which for long has prided itself in surviving so many crises, may at last have to acknowledge that it, too, is temporary in nature. Its task is to serve a larger reality, one that becomes much more coherent and challenging as global horizons expand at many different levels of life. All indications are that this will be a painful transition for all the churches. Mercifully, it may not be a prolonged illness, because the transition may be little more than a few decades away.

Bibliography:

Boff, Leonardo (1985), *Church, Charism and Power,* SCM Press.

Elliott, Charles (1985), *Praying the Kingdom: Towards a Political Spirituality,* Darton, Longman & Todd.

Fox, Matthew (1984), *Original Blessing: A Primer in Creation Spirituality,* New Mexico: Bear & Co. Inc.

Sheehan, Thomas (1986), *The First Coming: How the Kingdom of God Became Christianity,* Random House.

12

From Physical to Psychic Evolution

The universe does not exist 'out there' independent of us. We are inescapably involved in bringing about that which appears to be happening. We are not only observers. We are participators. In some strange sense this is a participatory universe.

John Archibald Wheeler

Most people today accept the notion of an evolving universe. In real life, however, people find it a bewildering and at times incomprehensible concept. If evolution means progress into higher and better ways of living, then why do most things in our world seem to be going desperately wrong. Why the continued warfare and political oppression? Why the ever-increasing exploitation and pollution of the environment? Why the unconquered – and apparently unconquerable – superiority of meaningless pain and suffering? While, theoretically, our universe is evolving we humans and the planet we inhabit seem to be regressing.

OUR EVOLUTIONARY STORY

It is easy to accept evolution as a notional or intellectual concept, as an idea in the *head:* to embrace it as a dimension of living experience – a feeling of the *heart* – demands not one but many conversions. For a start, evolution is a wholistic notion covering timespans that the human mind can barely grasp. What today we call the Big Bang – a single point of raw potential, bearing all matter, all dimension, all energy and all time, bursting out, spewing forth its contents, which already in the first hundredth of a second had formed the tiniest subatomic particles known to us today (eg. quarks and leptons) – is believed to have happened some thirteen billion years ago. About four and a half billion years ago, our planet spun away as an independent satellite in the solar system. Three billion years ago, with the appearance of the first algae, 'life' emerged on earth. Fish appeared four hundred million years ago, and two hundred million years later, the first mammals.

Human beings are relatively recent visitors to Planet Earth. A crude form of human life, about which we know relatively little, seems to have existed some fourteen million years ago. Our first trace of what we may consider a genuine human species is that of *Homo Habalis,* dated some two million years ago. The most recent categorisation, marking the evolution of contemporary human beings, is known as *Homo Sapiens Sapiens* (Linnaeus, 1758), now believed to have inhabited the earth for an estimated 40,000 years.

In this condensed summary, let us note a few crucial factors, which we tend to dismiss or take for granted:

1. Our universe was unfolding and evolving for eight and a half billion years before Planet Earth adopted an independent identity within the solar system. Although we have formally disowned the one time Christian conviction that the earth was the centre of the universe, and every other planet revolved around it, we still act and think as if we, the citizens of Planet Earth, have some type of monopoly over universal life. Scientists work feverishly to uncover the laws governing the universe; theologians spend an entire lifetime trying to unpack the mysteries of life; politicians consider outer space as conquerable territory for the benefit of Earth's citizens. Perhaps we need to hold our breath for a moment, simply to realize '. . . how little we are in it all.'

In the grand design – whatever its origin or destiny – could it be that there is a profound significance in the fact that Planet Earth has spent considerably more time in the womb of the universe than as an independent entity? To many readers – especially the more learned – this may seem a tantalisingly pointless idea. Not, I suggest, for one who is trying to understand our planet *wholistically* or in terms of quantum theory. We draw a parallel with the life of an unborn child. For many years the nine months in the womb was considered to be quite insignificant compared with the 'real' life, which commenced at birth. Progressively we are coming to realize that those nine months, right from the moment of conception, can have profound effects upon later growth and development, even into adult life.

I have no idea as to what is the cosmological, scientific or spiritual significance of the Earth's long pregnancy in the womb of the universe. I am not prepared to accept that it was sheer blind chance. I believe there was a reason and a purpose, which tentatively suggests that we cannot hope to understand Planet Earth until we learn a great deal more about the larger reality to which the Earth belongs, namely the universe itself.

2. Much more important is the fact that humans have inhabited Planet Earth for less than five per cent of its entire lifespan. In fact, *Homo Sapiens Sapiens* has been around for less than one per cent of that time. And yet we think and act, plan and exploit, as if *we* were the inventors of it all. It is a salutary lesson to realize that life in the universe, and on Planet Earth herself, unfolded in all its great range, variety and elegance without any assistance from humans for over ninety-five per cent of the earth's history.

I do not wish to suggest that we are unimportant to the planet. I do wish to assert that we have grossly exaggerated our importance, and continue to do so. We tend to think of ourselves as superior or juxtaposed to the rest of creation. We assume an exalted position which, in fact, alienates us from creation, an illusive superiority that becomes (as is apparent today) extremely self-destructive.

3. As the evolution of life unfolds, so does complexity and the power of mind. Prior to the existence of all known life-forms, very simple single-celled creatures inhabited our world. Life-forms became progressively more complex, more elegant and more mysterious in nature. Complexity as an evolutionary concept is not about things becoming more *complicated*. It is about life becoming capable of mutual enrichment through

diversity and variety. Thankfully, modern science is rediscovering the breadth and depth of richness in this concept; meanwhile, traditional religion continues to augment fear and suspicion of complexity.

An important aspect of this complexity is the power of *mind*. Here I use the term *mind* in a very ancient sense, incorporating *psyche* and *spirit* as well as mental powers (a sense re-echoed in Gregory Bateson's distinction between *mind* and *mentation*.) I am particularly intrigued by the debate about human thought-forms being superior to those of animals, or human feelings being different from those of plants. Instead I wish to suggest that the *thinking* and *feeling* potentials of life exhibit themselves differently in the variety of life-forms, because this would seem to be the most creative way for the mutual enrichment activated in the grand design of life, or in what Paul Davies (1988) has called the 'cosmic blueprint'.

According to this argument, consciousness is not a quality which humans possess in a manner or degree different from and superior to animals. That may be the actual situation, but its significance is discernible at a deeper, more wholistic level of understanding. The tendency today is to suggest that the universe becomes conscious in and through different life-forms, or perhaps, more accurately, the conscious potential of the universe realizes itself in the different forms of conscious expression. Accordingly, we must not and cannot assume that we are the final life-form in the evolutionary scale (an impression conveyed, consciously or unconsciously, in Brandon Carter's notion of the *Anthropic Principle:* cf. Barrow & Tipler, 1986). There is every reason to believe that higher forms of creature will emerge in future evolutionary unfolding throughout the millions – perhaps billions – of years yet to come.

EVOLUTION AND BECOMING

Teilhard de Chardin (1959, 1978) remains one of the most visionary and succinct thinkers on this question, mainly, I suggest, because of his ability to link scientific and spiritual insight. For De Chardin, evolution is a process of becoming (for which he uses terms like *genesis* and *cosmogenesis*). He describes the process in terms of 'stages' and 'progression', all leading to higher levels of complexity, which for De Chardin, is a primary manifestation of the divine energy at work in evolution (1959, p.43).

In the course of evolutionary development, Teilhard outlines the various stages:

(a) *Geogenesis:* the geological unfolding, leading to (b) *Biogenesis:* the various life forms, of which (c) *Psychogenesis* – the mental development of humankind – is the culminating stage, leading to (d) *Noogenesis:* the world becoming more conscious, in and through human consciousness, an universal state which De Chardin calls the *Noosphere.* (e) *Christogenesis* is considered to be the omega point of convergence, the final unification of all creation under God as head.

A great deal of de Chardin's thought and writing centres on the *Noosphere*. His unique and daring insight was that our universe had already entered the phase of *psychic* evolution, and consequently it was inappropriate to continue promoting a world view where material/physical thought and action patterns were considered superior to mental and spiritual orientations. In the *Noosphere,* we have moved not beyond, but into a whole new way (a higher level) of interacting with our universe, calling forth from us a response that is essentially spiritual and wholistic in its ambience and orientation.

These reflections enable us to address directly the transition we wish to explore in this chapter. It was Teilhard himself who hinted in the 1950s that physical evolution – of both the universe and humanity – had progressed just about as far as it could; that its next course of direction was beyond the physical, into the realm of psyche and spirit, and this I call *psychic* evolution.

I am not suggesting that the *physical* is no longer important. The challenge now facing us is to perceive and understand the physical in a whole new light, perhaps as matter striving to become conscious, not just in human beings, but in a whole variety of new ways, as yet largely unimaginable to the human intellect.

TWO CONCEPTS OF EVOLUTIONARY GROWTH

PHYSICAL	PSYCHIC
1. The planet consists of dead, inert matter. Materiality is the essence of life.	The planet is alive with consciousness. There is more to life than materiality.
2. The physical/material world is the only real one.	The physical/material world is one stage in the evolution of the universe.
3. Chance and necessity govern the evolution of life.	Evolution is marked by purpose, pattern and design.
4. In evolutionary terms, the essential nature – in this case, the physical – remains unchanged (cyclic/linear growth).	In wholistic terms, growth means transformation into higher, more complex levels of being (exponential growth).
5. All evolution culminates in the human species; we are the jewel in the crown.	We are not the final stage of evolution. In all probability, higher creatures will evolve in the future.
6. Man is the master of creation and will determine the future direction of evolution.	We humans are stewards of an evolving planet over which we do not have a monopoly of control.
7. Creation (by God) alone is real. Evolution is a human fabrication.	God continually co-creates in the *becoming* and begetting of life.
8. Life is getting more chaotic; instead of evolving we seem to be regressing.	Calvary precedes resurrection; creativity can also be born out of chaos.

9. Evolution is a vague, unscientific notion; there are too many unknowns.	We are dealing primarily with a spiritual unfolding that confounds all our laws and procedures.

BEYOND MATERIAL FORMS

There is much to suggest that this transition is taking place. In the field of information technology, we are now capable of containing massive amounts of information in tiny physical objects, namely microchips. What took a massive physical space a few hundred years ago is now reduced to a little object no bigger than one's thumb. There is a profound symbolism here, indicating that we are rapidly approaching the time when the physical container for information will become invisible to the human eye, initially some type of quark-like object (bearing in mind that physicists have never actually seen a quark), and eventually the storage of information in consciousness itself.

In 1977, for the first time in history, over half the USA workforce was involved in processing information. We have moved into the information era. Mind-stuff is becoming our daily diet; computers are becoming a type of global brain, while we humans continue to unfold into something akin to the nervous system of the planet.

Because physical and material means are failing to address the needs of our world, we are experiencing much chaos and confusion. Most governments still endorse – unconsciously for the greater part – the mechanistic view of life. As I write these words, the British chancellor of the exchequer is talking about the economy *overheating*. The language says it all. Playing around with the parts of the machine is archaic and inefficient; it is the old way of doing things; it simply doesn't work anymore!

To continue to play this game only frustrates and angers the people. Violence erupts; services break down; prices run out of control; we exploit resources; we pollute for selfish gain. It all sounds familiar, doesn't it? Why? Because the system we are operating – at all levels of life – is out of tune with the aspirations of our time.

The old system is crumbling and dying, with the anger, confusion and pain of every death experience. The negative response becomes all the more pronounced if we resist the transition – which is exactly what most people are doing. There is no purely physical or material solution to our contemporary global problems. The collective consciousness has shifted towards the supra-physical. Our only choice is to move forward with it, or otherwise die the slow and painful death which denial and resistance brings about.

THE TIME-SCALE OF CULTURAL EVOLUTION

Like most issues explored in this book, the shift towards psychic evolution became more obvious in the 1960s. We are therefore referring to a transition now twenty-five to thirty years old. This time-scale may be helpful in understanding many of the transitions I refer to, but for an evolutionary shift it is far too short a time span. Major evolutionary transitions are calculated in hundreds, perhaps thousands of years. The transition referred to in the present chapter is of a type occurring, perhaps, every 50,000 years, and taking at least a few centuries to make the shift from the old to the new.

Such transitions are not entirely new. The nineteenth-century French biologist, Georges Curvier, records *twenty-seven* such events. Yet we know very little about them. Only with hindsight can we register their occurrence, and then it is too late to record the actual experience for posterity. We are left, therefore, with a range of general statements, such as:

'If one looks back through any sequence of ancient fossil-bearing rocks, one notices a persistent theme: change. New species appear, while established ones vanish, but instead of showing a sequence of smooth transitions, the fossil record gives an impression that the changes happened in a series of jumps . . . The mechanisms by which species arise and subsequently slip into extinction have puzzled biologists for a very long time.'

(Leakey, 1981, p.22)

Past evolutionary shifts of global proportion tend to be attributed to severe climatic changes resulting in extensive glaciation or widespread flooding due to rise of temperature. Consequently, intervening periods between bursts of evolutionary unfolding are often referred to as Ice Ages. It is a tentative explanation, and far from satisfactory. Perhaps with the development of the new science of *chaos,* we may discover a whole new understanding of evolution, beset with interacting periods of chaos and order (cf. Gleick, 1988, p.170).

THE OLD IN THE NEW

For the time being, we live with the prospect of an impending evolutionary shift, which may or may not resemble former occurrences. While we don't seem to have much to learn from former experiences, it is at least reassuring to realize that these were events that projected the Earth into a new and more creative stage of development. We must note, however, that it was progress *at a price* – a costly measure of pain and suffering and the diminution, if not the extinction, of the old order of existence.

And yet the old order was not completely obliterated. In a sense, the old is contained in the new, albeit in a transformed fashion. In fact in a time of evolutionary shift, the old and new seem to mingle in strangely mysterious ways. Cultural historians such as Toynbee, Danilevsky, Spengler and Sorokin all describe the transition phase as one of chaos, disintegration, struggle and hardship. People tend to behave in tribalistic fashion; the old law and order has broken down; the new system has not yet come to fruition.

Anthropologists name this experience one of *recapitulation,* and it seems to be significantly important for a coherent interpretation of what is happening in today's world. Apparently, in cultural transitions, the movement from the old to the new tends to follow the pattern of the long-jumper athlete who takes twenty steps back in order to leap thirty paces forward. Each new evolutionary wave brings with it the cumulative wealth of each former one, but also activates the primal, archetypal, instinctive value system of our species (in the case of human evolution). This is not a return to infantile, primitive, tribalistic chaos – although on the surface it may seem so – but to the mythic simplicity and fraternity (the tribe/clan) of the primitives, untouched by the conditioning and enculturation of later developments.

The process of recapitulation is quite complex, and may have fuelled a great deal of the hippie/dropout behaviour of the 1960s, and the more recent trends in crime, immorality, and the rejection of standard societal values. The tendency towards 'neo-tribalism' may be the strongest 'proof' of the evolutionary transition depicted in these pages. As the old order dies and the new yearns to be born, the collective unconscious seeks to reconnect with primordial inspiration, not for the sake of infantile regression, but as an added impetus to capitulate us into a totally new future.

Bibliography:

De Chardin, Teilhard (1959), *The Phenomenon of Man,* London: Collins.

(1978), *The Heart of Matter,* London: Collins.

Gleick, James (1988), *Chaos: Making a New Science,* Heinemann.

Leakey, Richard E. (1981). *The Making of Mankind,* New York: E.P. Dutton.

Barrow, John D. & Tipler, Frank J. (1986), *The Anthropic Cosmological Principle,* Oxford: Clarendon Press.

PART THREE

POLARISATION:
IN THE THICK OF BATTLE

Denial, however human and natural a response, exacts a terrible price.

Marilyn Ferguson

Chance favours the prepared mind.

Alexander Fleming

Transition is a rather illusive term. It may give the impression of a gentle progressive movement from one state of affairs to another. This is often the case, but not for the evolutionary shifts explored in this book.

What I have briefly outlined is a series of cultural shifts, from an established state of affairs to an emerging, as yet ill-defined, vision of the future. Firstly, we need to note that this is something that has not been planned, engineered or pioneered by humanity. We have not set up agencies or delegated governments to bring about this new state of affairs. Most of us, most of the time, get on with life in our day-to-day existence. Even when our living conditions are far from satisfactory, we feel comfortable with what we know and experience, and often we resist change, even though we know we'd be better off as a result.

In a sense, therefore, the transition(s) I describe is not of our own making. Although we did not set out *consciously* to activate it, we unconsciously contribute to its emergence. Every time we explore new ways of organising an event (whether a family party or an international conference), discover a new medicine, invent a new brand of food, uncover a fresh understanding on any aspect of life, marvel and rejoice at

137

beauty, we abandon something of the old and create a type of morphic resonance (a threshold of consciousness) that moves all mankind towards a novel perception of life. There are, therefore, subtle but powerful ways in which most of us, most of the time, yearn for something new, fresh, a more genuine and wholesome way of living (cf. Watson, 1989).

THE CLASH OF CULTURES

What happens at an evolutionary threshold is that these two movements – the tendency towards stability and the desire for innovation – interact in new ways. Normally, the dominant culture of the status quo is firmly in charge and feels capable – via its governments and institutions – of accommodating and controlling all the events and experiences of the body politic. In a time of transition, the body politic is unsure of its direction, apathetic about public policy, uneasy with strategic developments. A counter culture begins to emerge, and continues to gain strength and approval to the point where the mainstream culture can no longer contain it. Now the status quo feels threatened by the new movement; it subconsciously perceives an enemy at the gate, perhaps more powerful than itself!

The transition has become something of a battle of wits, a scenario depicted with great clarity by the sociologist Pitrim Sorokin (1950, p.297):

> 'My studies led to the generalisation that in the great crisis of transition from the declining old to the new emerging super-system, the polarisation of human souls, groups and values regularly occurs. Most persons and groups, who under normal conditions are neither too saintly nor too sinful, who render to Caesar what is Caesar's and to God what is God's, tend in the conditions of catastrophe or crisis to polarise. Some become more saintly, more religious, more ethical; others more sinful, more atheistic, more cynical than before. The positive, religious-ethical polarisation appears as a renaissance of religion and ethics, noted by

138

Spengler and others. Factually, in the period of transition the full picture is growth, not only of religiosity and morality but of irreligiosity and demoralisation. Only later on, when the new cultural supersystem emerges, does the positive polarisation prevail and make the first phase of an emerging civilisation ethically strong and noble.'

Little wonder that the philosopher A.N. Whitehead could say with such conviction and cogency that the major advances in civilisation are processes that all but wreck the societies in which they occur. Although our world has undergone an estimated *twenty-seven* major evolutionary shifts, we seem to have learned very little from those traumatic experiences. As a species, we have a very poor sense of history; consequently, we continue to condemn ourselves by repeating the errors of former times.

Perhaps it's not too late to throw some historical light on the impending cultural crisis of our time, one that is likely to become much more pronounced as we move into the twenty-first century. We cannot date accurately the onset of the transition(s) outlined in this book. In part, they can be traced to the rise of Darwinianism and Marxism in the nineteenth century, and to the scientific discoveries (relativity and quantum theory) at the beginning of the twentieth century. As a broad cultural force, however, their main impact commenced in the 1960s. A restlessness began to pervade our world; people posed questions and discussed topics formerly reserved to specialists; we travelled to the four corners of Planet Earth and even as far as the moon; we allowed ourselves to be shocked by the poverty and pollution of our world, and we registered our disapproval by protest and solidarity. The powers of Church or State had little idea what was happening; they assumed that these freakish upsurges would fade away; and to the extent that these trends are still around, the institutions either ignore or dismiss them.

What we have failed to realize is that the events of the 1960s were the symptoms of a major cultural transition, probably a major evolutionary shift. Up to that time people lived in relatively isolated pockets called *nations;* even within individual countries, many people never travelled more than a hundred miles from home. Lifestyle and custom were structured and stylised, passed on almost unaltered from one generation to the next. Most of humanity lived a type of cocoon existence, largely oblivious to the wider world.

Then came television, global travel, mass communications, along with the new trends and revolutionary stirrings of the 1960s. Most people didn't realize what had hit them; many still don't. Some marvelled and wondered; others were intrigued. A minority, mainly the young, joined the bandwagon, much to the annoyance and disgust of their elders.

Thirty years later, we are beginning to come to grips with the events of the 1960s. It has taken us thirty years to do so, and in terms of evolutionary progress, that is quite an achievement. To break out of the claustrophobic cocoon of the pre-1960s and allow ourselves to be changed by our changing world is no easy transition to have made. This is what people are grappling with today.

COPING WITH CHANGE

In fact, people *have* changed – they had no other option! By and large the changes have been superficial, and in most cases, we have no feeling or understanding for what caused the change, or on where it might be leading us now; for the past few decades we have been drifting along. My hope is that a book of this nature will enable more people to *participate consciously* in this new evolutionary thrust, so that the long-term experience is one of breakthrough rather then breakdown.

In our world today, we can identify three broad groups of change-agents, adopting either the strategy of *dialogue, resistance* or *drift:*

1. Those who try to *dialogue* with change respect it for what it is, and try to flow with its momentum. These are the people envisaged by Sorokin when he refers to the new cultural supersystem. They may be people who are grossly dissatisfied with the politics and economics of our time, but feel powerless to do anything about it, or those disillusioned with our

religious institutions and feel they can no longer remain within. Or they may be people who have taken more radical options and have become active in women's movements, CND, ecology and environmental groups, cooperative experiments, human rights campaigners, alternative communities, Green politics or a range of other marginalised ventures.

2. Secondly, there are those who *resist* change, what Sorokin calls the old declining supersystem. Most governments of State and Church – with the possible exception of Gorbachev's *perestroika* – adopt this stance. They do so in good faith, believing that most people want law and order along with a neat and efficient sociopolitical system. But increasing numbers of 'ordinary' people are losing faith in the political/ ecclesiastical system. Less than fifty per cent of the American electorate voted for either Presidents Reagan or Bush, while in the Christian churches, less than twenty per cent attend regularly. The major institutions have largely lost the rank-and-file of society; in fact, the rift would be more pronounced were it not for the subtle manipulation whereby institutions create a dependency (as with unemployed people) which obliges people to remain within the system.

In resisting the change, our major institutions are defending their own space rather than safeguarding people against alien forces. Institutions are powerfully self-perpetuating, and in the face of change will compel allegiance in subtle and devious ways, exploiting the weak into further dependence and eliciting the favour of the rich by increasing benefits. It is all a ploy for not having to look at the harsh and messy reality that is endemic to every major cultural change.

3. The bulk of the people *drift;* they are carried along by the sweep of change, disillusioned at times, frequently disorient-ated but resigned to the fact that 'this is the way things are'. The tragedy here is the lack of appropriate awareness: *people do not understand what's going on!* In becoming enlightened and informed, they are empowered to make choices. Without this awareness, they are in danger of being sucked into a whirlwind of polarisation, with the two powerful forces of

change swaying to the right and to the left.

NAMING THE WHIRLWIND

There is nothing wrong with the polarisation in itself; it is endemic to cultural change. If we know what's going on, then the chances are that we will not get ensnared in the whirlwind; if we are unaware of what is happening, we become enmeshed in resistant behaviour, in which we exert much energy in the denial and projection that classically accompanies such change. The work of Kubler-Ross (1970) on the human resistances to death (through the stages of denial, anger, bargaining, depression and acceptance) is immensely helpful in understanding this quality of response and enabling us to move beyond it (cf. O'Murchú, 1987, pp.35ff).

Polarisation is unavoidable. It is the darkness of the Calvary experience that precedes resurrection. Like the Jesus of Christianity, we cannot avoid Calvary; we go *through* it to the dawn and hope of Easter. So much of the pain and misery in our world today is not caused by those who strive to move with the transition (an accusation frequently made by those guarding the status quo), but by the masses, who are oblivious to what is happening and inadvertently contribute to the cultural resistance which creates the polarisation in the first place. *Enlightenment,* that great Buddhist virtue, is the most urgently-needed commodity of our time.

I owe a great deal of my own understanding to Fritjof Capra, whose book *The Turning Point* provides a superb exposition of the polarisation taking place in today's world. His concluding paragraphs focus on this very subject, and his final remarks are an apt conclusion to the material of this section and to the vision I have outlined in the present work:

'During the process of decline and disintegration the dominant social institutions are still imposing their outdated views but are gradually disintegrating, while new creative minorities face the new challenges with ingenuity and rising confidence.
    '. . . While the transformation is taking place, the

declining culture refuses to change, clinging ever more rigidly to its outdated ideas; nor will the dominant social institutions hand over their leading roles to the new cultural forces. But they will inevitably go on to decline and disintegrate while the rising culture will continue to rise, and eventually will assume its leading role. As the turning point approaches the realisation that evolutionary changes of this magnitude cannot be prevented by short-term political activities provides our strongest hope for the future.'

(Capra, 1982, p.466)

Bibliography:

Capra, Fritjof (1982), *The Turning Point,* Flamingo paperback.

Kubler-Ross, Elizabeth (1970), *On Death and Dying,* Tavistock & Methuen.

O'Murchú, Diarmuid (1987), *Coping With Change in the Modern World,* Cork: Mercier Press & Leominster: Fowler Wright.

Sorokin, Pitrim (1950), *Modern Historical and Social Philosophies,* New York: Dover Publications.

Watson, Lyall (1989), *Neophilia: The Tradition of the New,* Sceptre Books.

EPILOGUE

Reweaving the Tapestry of Change

According to our rational way of thinking, change is something we humans initiate, control and wield to our own advantage and to that of life universally. Whether Christian or not, we cling to the notion that we are *masters* of the universe and are capable of determining its destiny (cf. Gen. 1:28). We can choose what is going to happen, make it happen in a way that best serves our wishes and modify the dynamics as circumstances demand. Manipulation and control are the secret tools to effect this process.

And we have created a series of institutions that enable us to attain our targets. Foremost among these is the political structure, which tends to be democratic or autocratic. In either case, power has been delegated to the selected few on behalf of the masses. Socio-economic considerations are the primary focus of political activity, and in not a few cases today the pioneers of social and economic policy (the civil servants and their advisors) are really the ones who dictate changing values and life patterns. Economists, more than any other grouping, command supreme power in today's world; verily, it is money that makes the world go round!

On the socio-economic front, the multinational corporations outstrip governments in altering and dictating fiscal and human values, but few governments will openly acknowledge this fact. The corporations are accountable to nobody, apart from themselves. They wield a power and influence unmatched in any previous historical epoch.

In the traditional tapestry of change, two other institutions exert significant influence‘ *religion* and *labour*. Apart from Islam, *religion* today rarely impacts strongly upon either personal life or political activity. Christianity is prevalent in parts of the West, and in Central and South America; Hinduism is widely practised in India, but in all these situations, religious practice is diminishing and its influence is waning. Islam, alone among the major religions, is actually extending its influence, and one wonders how long such an archaic and barbaric belief-system can continue to thrive on human gullibility, ignorance and insecurity.

Labour, as a major change agent, assumes a very different dynamic in varying sectors of Planet Earth. The Marxist conviction that real power is invested in the working class and is best invoked through constructive social organisation has strongly influenced the West; the trade union movement still adheres to this ideology, although it has waned considerably in recent years. In Asia, Africa and southern America (often lumped together as 'the Third World'), work patterns are immensely diversified, largely devoid of technological skill and more oriented towards cooperation than towards competition. Moreover, the lucrative value of Third World resources – even to this day – is largely exploited and usurped by Western political and economic forces.

This general overview is more than sufficient to challenge the rather intransigent rational argument that we humans know what's going on in today's world and are still pretty much in charge. We may be losing the battle (note the metaphor) against poverty, corruption, world debt, etc. *but we'll get there eventually!* And occasionally one hears the pathetic, blasphemous rationalisation: 'When all else fails, we know that God is on our side.' *Denial* is rampant in today's world. It is undoubtedly the single greatest outrage of our time.

The old world order – the domain of rational thought and patriarchal prowess – is in a shambles. Everything is breaking at the seams (see Drucker, Handy). Our political institutions become increasingly incompetent and anachronistic; economists waffle their way with words that bemuse and confuse even their own adherents, desperately trying to cover over their appalling ignorance (see Hamilton). Religion has become yet another patriarchal dinosaur dragging in its wake a long-lost understanding of human and planetary life.

Meanwhile, the ordinary woman and man, going about

their daily business, try to maintain a semblance of sanity and control. Many suspect that things have got dangerously out of hand on Planet Earth, but it feels too scary to look closely. Better pretend that all is well – or will be – and get on with life. What's the point in ruminating over all this negative stuff, particularly when there's nothing we ordinary folk can do about it!

The point is that all is not negative. There is another side that the rational, patriarchal mode of perception can neither understand nor appreciate, and therein lies real hope for the future. In this alternative consciousness lies the wisdom and hope for a new and better future. Beyond rationality lies a more creative mode innate to the process of evolution itself. It has sustained life and meaning over many millennia – well beyond the two thousand years of so-called civilisation – and once more assumes a central role if we are to evolve beyond our present crisis into the new world that's struggling to be born in our time.

I wish to outline some of the main features of the newly emerging world view, developments of recent decades that have gradually seeped into the mainstream consciousness. As we move into the new millennium, these elements are likely to emerge as the cultural nerve-points of our global evolutionary shift, and will become the threads that will enable us to weave a new cultural tapestry. I refer to six dominant developments:

1. The Integration of Chaos
2. The Polarity of Light and Darkness
3. The Rediscovery of the Feminine
4. Cosmology as the Primary Revelation
5. The Call to Outgrow Anthropocentrism
6. Learning to Perceive Laterally.

THE INTEGRATION OF CHAOS

Ever since the publication of Prigogine & Stingers' seminal work *Order Out of Chaos* in 1984, chaos theory has come to dominate many fields of contemporary wisdom. Interestingly, it is the physical sciences (Physics, Chemistry and, to a lesser extent, Biology) which lead the way in this new development, with the social sciences – especially in their managerial and consultancy expertise – gradually accommodating the new insights. Even some theologians include the theory in their explorations (e.g. Arbuckle, McDonagh). While some economists readily – even enthusiastically – espouse chaos theory, politicians are notably resistant. So indeed are the leaders of all major institutions: political, social and ecclesiastical.

Chaos theory offers two divergent approaches to enable us to comprehend and address the decline and breakdown of values, mores and standard behaviours in our contemporary world. Some scholars suggest that the two approaches are complementary rather than opposed to each other. Those who follow the Prigogine-Stingers school of thought suggest that for systems to operate creatively conditions must be such that newness and difference is accommodated. Every time new elements enter the system, there is a shuffling around (a turbulence) of what is already there; instability becomes the norm. The restlessness may reach points of extreme unease and disorganisation and then, perhaps quite suddenly and unpredictably, the whole system 'flips' into another mode of operating; a new and fresh sense of order ensues. The system progresses (grows) to a fresh level of attainment and achievement. The chaos (disorder) is a precondition for fresh order, following a developmental (evolutionary) process that nobody fully understands.

The second dominant approach, popularised by James Gleick, claims that chaotic behaviour is *inherent* in all living, dynamic (changing) systems, whether it be the human body or the cosmos at large. It is an integral dimension that is largely unpredictable and manifests in such ways as irregular weather patterns, the dripping of water taps, the filibrations of the human heart, the jagged nature of coastlines, which when measured with the aid of fractal mathematics, manifests a deep 'invisible' pattern beneath the 'visible' disorderly shapes. Similar to the Prigogine-Stingers school of thought, this latter group also claims that the creativity and elegance of the system is activated and sustained much more dynamically by the 'chaos' than by the 'order'. Chaos is inherent to the deeper meaning of life and indeed essential to comprehending life in its multifaceted dimensions (see Swimme & Berry).

In this time of complex and profound change, chaos abounds. It touches our daily lives in issues such as the loss of employment, the breakdown of relationships, the rise in crime, the numerous uncertainties about the future, the discarding of traditionally cherished values. Where we allow these experiences to touch us deeply ' and most people don't do this – then life begins to feel precarious and quite frightening; hence, the alarming increase in suicides in recent years.

Not many years ago, such troubled moments could be assuaged by a visit to the doctor, a consultation with one's MP, a session with the bank manager, a chat with the local priest or vicar or some quiet days on Retreat. But today, many of these outlets exacerbate rather than reassure: the wise gurus, whether it be the bank manager, the parliamentarian, the doctor or the priest, know no better than the rest of us. In fact, because of their reliance on traditional, patriarchal wisdom, the 'experts' are often more confused than we ourselves are – and frequently, our innate, human wisdom tells us precisely that.

So, where do we turn? Spiritual gurus, particularly those seasoned in the great spiritual traditions of our world, offer advice that may have within it greater substance than we initially care to recognise: *turn within, reconnect with your own inner 'heart'. From that still point learn to befriend the chaos and, whatever else you do, don't run away from it!* Indeed, it is only from within a spiritual context (and not necessarily a *religious* one – see Chapter Five) that this advice makes any sense. We live in a spiritually impoverished world; so, sadly, many people are unable to make this connection. And this observation leads to the next dominant thread in our attempt to reweave the tapestry of change.

THE POLARITY OF LIGHT AND DARKNESS

Imagine for a moment a clear sky on a summer's day. The sun is shining brightly and you are standing in an open space, close to a huge, fully-leafed tree. You will readily notice that the stronger the sun shines, then the darker the shadow that

148

will ensue from the tree.

This is a paradox with several important applications. Philosophically, it claims that light and shadow are complementary sides of life; the one needs the other for its expression and realisation. Jungian psychology has developed this insight with remarkable ingenuity, not merely at the level of personal growth and integration, but also in terms of planetary and cosmic processes; I refer to what Jungians call the Collective Unconscious.

In a sense, this is another rendition of chaos theory and helps to explicitate its deeper meaning. It is often suggested – spiritually and psychologically – that the crisis moments of our lives have a rich potential for growth and new meaning, if handled by enlightened guides. Pain and sickness can be experiences of transformation, begetting a whole new understanding of, and empathy for, oneself and others. We are dealing with a process that the rational mind, operating in isolation, can neither understand nor appropriate.

Nor have the major religions contributed to a creative interaction of those often opposing forces. All the major faiths endorse a *dualistic* view of life whereby the divine is opposed to the human, the spirit to the body, good to evil. Dualisms are constructs of our human mind rather than objective descriptions of reality. The dualistic mind-set belongs to the era of patriarchy when we humans (the male in particular) set out to conquer and control the then inhabited world. This process began about 10,000 years ago with the rise of the Agricultural Revolution and has continued, more or less unabated, to the present time. The philosophy of patriarchy is predominantly one of *divide and conquer.* Consequently, for every perceived 'good' there must be an opposing 'evil'. What is deemed good or evil is largely determined by the perception and intention of the dominating force.

The patriarchal urge to divide and conquer takes on a particular dualistic focus in the prevailing Greek thought of the final millennium prior to Christianity. It is primarily from this Greek source that Western culture has inherited the dualistic mode, which surfaces strongly in all subsequent religious and political praxis.

The polarity of light and darkness dominates Christian thought, with the darkness always depicted as deviant, destructive, valueless and embodied in a supernatural personification, called Satan. This depiction requires a stronger force of light that engages in battle with the evil force, in a contest that will only culminate at 'the end of time'. The battle between light and darkness is the ultimate aberration of our patriarchal culture which seeks to dominate and eliminate all that cannot be conquered and controlled by the masculine will-to-power.

The task of re-integrating the shadow – those instinctual, wild, erotic, creative, often destructive forces (whether personal or planetary) – is a supreme political and spiritual challenge for our time. Life needs both in order to attain its fullest potential. Instead of the dualistic either/or, we need to embrace afresh the challenging engagement of the both-and. Black holes serve as an intriguing example for the integration of the light-darkness duality. Black holes are considered to be the ultimate encapsulation of destruction and disintegration. Nothing can escape the absorbing power of a black hole. It sucks in everything that comes within its reach, and that which is ingested is lost for ever in a fathomless pit.

Scientific investigation of the past few decades suggests, however, that black holes may not be as deadly as once assumed. The complicated mathematics – the language with which scientists strive to make sense out of many processes – suggest an as yet untapped resourcefulness in black-hole activity. It seems possible that tiny particles such as photons come sufficiently close to the mouth of a black hole to be affected by its energy but can escape before being sucked in, thus bearing vital information, not just about the hole itself but possibly about initial conditions at the beginning of space-time.

More fascinating still is the recent suggestion that what goes into a black hole may come out in a transformed fashion at another moment in the space-time continuum. Thus, black holes may be the birthplace for energy-connections known as white holes or worm holes, giving birth to baby universes which in time may become as elegant and developed as our own universe (see Hawking. 1993).

These ruminations are not based on mere speculation. The elegant mathematics indicate a serious pursuit, still very much in its infancy. It may well provide the crucial evidence we need if we are to take seriously the power and potential of what many of the great mystics call the *via negativa,* the dark night of the soul, or the senses, those experiences of darkness, alienation, abandonment and meaninglessness which fuel and complement the evolutionary, universal drive towards a wholeness that transforms rather than destroys the darkness (see especially Swimme & Berry).

THE CALL TO OUTGROW ANTHROPOCENTRISM

The irrational urge towards the dualism of divide and conquer begets the idolatrous ideology of anthropocentrism. For some 10,000 years now, we humans have assumed (subconsciously, for the greater part) that reality is as we perceive it to be, or as we seek to determine it. Everything is measured and named from a *human* perspective. What we humans consider to be the state of our world, or anything in it, is the way it is, or should be. This insatiable urge underpins the Old Testament notion that we humans are intended to be the *masters* of creation (Gen. 1:28). It also undergirds monotheism (the belief in one supreme God) as the only valid religious belief, because it validates all human hierarchies in their task of conquering and controlling. In a sense, therefore, the monotheistic religions themselves – Judaism, Christianity and Islam – are supremely destructive forms of idolatry.

The anthropocentric urge seems to have emerged with the Agricultural Revolution about 8000 BC. Prior to that time, humans seem to have lived and behaved in a much more cooperative and equalitarian mode, befriending the planet (and the cosmos) in its evolutionary trajectory, rather than trying to manipulate everything from a human point of view. (More on this in Eisler.) The Agricultural Revolution generated a will-to-power, leading progressively to the fragmentation of our planet into what we now call nation states, tribal groups, ethnic collectives and major religions. To enforce the divide-and-conquer philosophy, we invented *warfare,* and the tragic consequences of that development are all too blatant in our world today.

The so-called 'scientific method' or 'religious dogma' are examples of anthropocentrism, whereby objective truth is

151

perceived as belonging to a higher wisdom, but is effectively nothing more than human speculation. There often follows perposterous judgements whereby rational logic leads to grossly convoluted conclusions. Take, for example, the research on the DNA spiral, of which we understand in depth little more than 3 per cent with an increasing awareness of the role of a further 10 per cent. The remaining 87 per cent scientists often arrogantly and ruthlessly dismiss as *junk DNA.* Just because *Homo Sapiens,* at this juncture of our evolutionary development, can't detect or determine DNA's meaning or purpose, we proceed to play 'God' and dismiss what *we* can't conquer as junk. No room is left for future research or understanding and there is not the faintest acknowledgement that, in due course, a more highly evolved and enlightened species will probably unravel quite easily the as yet undiscovered secrets of DNA.

The future of our planetary survival remains dangerously poised while we humans continue to adopt a stringent, anthropomorphic outlook. We are the masters of neither creation nor evolution. We are an inherent part of the co-creative process, not an alien force set in opposition to the rest of creation. Our role would seem to be, as Swimme & Berry suggest, that of supreme *listeners* and not supreme *doers.*
Listening has a bad press in our anthropomorphic culture. It is perceived to be passive, weak and ineffectual. It is something children should do at home or at school; that people should do at conferences or at training courses; that employers should do in the presence of employees. Those who have the right to speak are perceived to possess the power, and, therefore, do not have to listen; in fact, they rarely do.

No other quality is so urgently needed today. Millions cry out to be heard, to be listened to, to be allowed some say in a harsh and brutal world. Planet Earth itself cries out amid its pain of pollution, exploitation and desecration at the hands of barbaric, anthropomorphic manipulators who continue to 'torture nature 'til she reveals her last secrets to us,' (Francis Bacon). Politically, economically and spiritually our world yearns for a whole new way of being. We need to listen to the groans and aspirations that come from deep within.

CREATION AS THE PRIMARY REVELATION

The call to outgrow our anthropomorphic addiction to power and destruction demands a radical evaluation, not merely of what humanity is meant to be about, but also what the cosmos itself is about. The notion of our world (especially Planet Earth) being a cold, inanimate object to be conquered and controlled, not merely begets a pointless universe, but also casts humanity in a role of ultimate self-destruction. The pursuit of the ultimate building blocks, in what is perceived to be a mechanistic universe, is proving to be a dead end. The deeper we plunge, the more illusive our vision becomes and the more elegant and mysterious is the universe we encounter.

Relatively recent discoveries, like the vastness of empty space (the creative vacuum) and the halo of dark matter in the far reaches of time-space, suggest an enormously complex and, as yet, largely unknown universe. The growing awareness that Planet Earth is better construed as a living organism (the Gaia hypothesis) rather than as a mechanical object, demands that we learn to relate with our Earth in a subject-to-subject partnership rather than in an object-to-object competitive contest. And our deepening understanding of the process of evolution reveals an universe of profound mystery and enormous vitality, the greater reality of which we humans – at this stage of our evolution – can only grasp in a meagre way.

Spiritually, modern cosmology poses a profound and provocative challenge, namely that the universe itself, and not the religions, is the primary source of revelation. It is in the unfolding orchestra of creation that we feel and intuit (as our pre-historic ancestors did for thousands of years) a divine presence, fundamentally creative and benign in nature. In the evolving dance of creation, we connect with the divine life-force that permeates existence in its entirety. Some theorists underplay the evolutionary story, indeed, some question its very existence, because of so many unknowns – and particularly because of those huge gaps in our knowledge regarding certain evolutionary epochs. Once again, our anthropomorphic blindness gets in the way. Because we cannot detect a rational, sequential progressive unfolding across the millennia. We question even the possibility of evolution itself. If the universe is the primary revelation and is characterised by an amazing propensity for self-organisation and self-renewal, then surely it can attend to its own self-development without our participation or engagement at every step of the way. In fact, it has evolved without any human assistance for some fifteen billion years, maybe even for considerably longer.

Once again, we need to recall what we said in the last section: our human role is not about controlling or directing the whole creative enterprise, but *listening* and attending to the ongoing revelation. Our primary task is not to dominate life, but to celebrate it – in love and justice. The late Karl Rahner suggested that God reveals in accordance with our capacity to receive revealed truth (wisdom). If we ourselves continue to play God, to manipulate the will-to-power totally and solely in anthropomorphic terms, then little wonder that we live in such a godless world. The central religious problem of our time is that most of our religious Gods are false ones, alien to and alienated from the meaning of life and evolution.

When we reclaim the creation itself as the primary creative energy of life (whether we deem it divine or not), then not merely do our actions change, but so do our attitudes and perceptions. When we assume our participatory role as creative listeners, we realise that the appropriate action is to flow with the creative process and not to hinder it because of vested interests of an outdated and highly dangerous will-to-power. In that challenging moment of conversion (not from the world but to it) and letting go, we'll discover afresh our true role: *to co-create attentively with our profoundly creative universe.*

THE REDISCOVERY OF THE FEMININE

The patriarchal urge to dominate and control is often described as a *masculine* life-force. It manifests as an intense, irrational desire to be fully in charge, with nothing left to chance; in other words, with little or no room for spontaneity and creativity. The feminine (as already indicated in Chapter Nine) is characterised by a readiness to flow with experience, to risk, to listen, to protect, to cherish life in its beauty, delicacy and diversity.

All humans, whether male or female, are endowed with both masculine and feminine characteristics. However, because of the one-sided influence of patriarchy, men have borne the brunt of the masculine will-to-power, and the impact of patriarchy tends to be internalised by women rather than by men. In their bodies and spirits, women feel and articulate the oppression that the conquering male has sought to impose upon people and planet alike.

Feminism, therefore, attempts not merely a restoration of balance; rather, it invokes a whole new way of relating to life, one that seeks to integrate both masculine and feminine energies in mutual interaction. To the powers of patriarchy, which still dominate (particularly in the Western world), work aimed at reclaiming the feminine poses a huge threat. Power is called to be accountable; power is challenged to share, to care, to cherish and, above all, to let go of its monopoly of interference and domination.

When patriarchal institutions are challenged, they react in one of two predictable ways:

a) **Denial:** Pretend that all is well and ignore the critics.
b) **Projection** (Blame): Accuse the critic of being uninformed, or simply unenlightened; or, alternatively, accuse the disturber of 'betrayal' and thus inculcate feelings of guilt.

Admission that the patriarchal mode might be wrong or inappropriate for our time, or that it has simply outlived its usefulness, is virtually unthinkable. Weakness, failure, 'shadow' is rarely acknowledged, and never engaged with. Thus, there tends to ensue a resolute polarisation between the masculine and feminine modes, a phenomenon all too familiar in the times in which we live.

Normally, the polarisation moves in the direction of outright deadlock. The defenders of power and 'orthodoxy' become more and more entrenched. Meanwhile, the alternative rising consciousness continues to strike root, and what once seemed a maverick and insubstantial movement continues to grow until in time it assumes a leading role. A paradigm shift has taken place and a whole new way of dealing with reality has become, or is in the process of becoming, normative.

In attempting to name the current paradigm, contemporary writers suggest that the dominant shift is from the declining mechanistic culture of the Industrial Revolution, with the machine as the dominant metaphor, to the emerging wholistic vision for which the holon is the central metaphor. Theorists suggest that we are well into this shift, although as yet it has not impinged seriously upon our world. The transition under consideration may need to be understood in a larger context, originating with the Agricultural Revolution (the birth of modern patriarchy) about 10,000 years ago and thus needing a few more centuries to decline to the point of being no longer able or appropriate to serve our deeper needs as a people and as a planet. The upsurge of the feminine, therefore, is only in its embryonic stage. Its real potential – of creativity and imagination – is yet to be realised. A chaotic, but immensely energising force, will be let loose upon the world.

LEARNING TO PERCEIVE LATERALLY

There are tapestries wherein the pattern(s) follows a recognisable sequence; there are others where no obvious patterns are discernible and there are others still which, like fractal images, display an elegance and beauty which cannot be reduced to, nor described by, any set of specific patterns. These latter images defy the logic and rationality of our linear mind-sets – the desire to construe reality in neat, manageable packages. They evoke a new mode of perception and intuition, popularly called the lateral mode.

Laterally-minded people go first for the big picture and seek the meaning of each constituent part from within the context of the greater whole. The lateral mind (*heart*, to be more accurate) extrapolates meaning, not from the obvious but from the elements that are likely to provide the greatest surprise. The lateral pursuit is not for what is readily observable, but for the as-yet-undiscovered, not because it will add to what we already know or perceive, but because it may well provide a whole new way of understanding.

Intuition and imagination, rather than rationality and verification, characterise the lateral mode. Meaning and purpose are embodied, not merely in the functioning of independent, autonomous parts, but in the interaction of those parts that brings about relationship or interconnectedness. In large measure, the lateral mode has been evoked not because we chose to employ it, but because the interdependent nature of contemporary life requires it. Nothing can be understood any more in autonomous isolation.

Change – whether at the micro or macro levels – cannot be reduced to the abandonment of an old model or lifestyle for the sake of a better one. Change is a process of transition and transformation. In most cases, change is instigated by factors inherent in the system itself, and in an open-ended planet, is a living, self-organising, self-renewing system. An outside manipulative agent is not necessary to instigate a process of change. To comprehend the changing evolution, therefore, we need a mode of understanding that can include and integrate factors that cannot be understood or explained solely on *rational* terms – hence the need for the lateral mode.

Just as we often cannot detect or determine how the process of change is initiated, neither can we control its eventual outcome. We use the word *transformation* to describe, not the final result, but the altered state of affairs that ensues, and may continue to ensue for quite a long time. Transformations need not always produce wholesome results; indeed, they may lead to the total destruction of a system, as has happened to many industrial enterprises (under the impact of technology and computerisation) in recent decades. For something new to be born, the old may have to diminish; in fact, it may need to become totally extinct. In spiritual language, we describe the process as that of birth-death-rebirth.

Without the ability to perceive laterally – to hold in one's consciousness an overview of all the elements and all the processes, including the negatives – we cannot hope to understand, in a meaningful way, the nature of contemporary change and the amorphous and complex tapestry it reweaves, not once but several times over, and at a rapidity unknown to previous generations. For example, computer technology multiplied *one-thousandfold* between 1970 and 1990. How can one internalise this awareness and not be overwhelmed by its enormity?

How can we acquire this lateral orientation? How can we internalise it for the benefit of both ourselves and future generations? Here we need to confront pedagogical questions of urgent ethical import. Evolution seems to be pushing this new consciousness upon us, and through their openness and ingenuity many people are acquiring this new wisdom. Yet our Western educational system continues to promote a linear, rational, competitive approach that feeds the patriarchal, capitalistic infrastructure of an outdated culture. Attempts at alternative educational systems, e.g. Montessori, Steiner, struggle even to survive, never mind gain formal recognition. Not only is the formal educational system largely irrelevant to the emerging consciousness and archaic in its central convictions, but its underlying subconscious motivation is highly dangerous and ethically untenable. But because it is such a powerful cultural system – and in most cases a very closed one – it is extremely difficult to confront and challenge its deleterious impact.

Perhaps our greatest hope rests in the power of the lateral mode itself to surface where it will and gain ground through its own inherent credibility. When this begins to happen on a sufficiently large scale, hopefully cracks will begin to show in the limited and limiting world of linear consciousness. Presumably it will only be in the face of extreme breakdown that the guardians of our educational system will see the folly and potential destructibility of the current paradigm.

CONCLUSION

To reweave the new tapestry of change we need threads from many looms, some of which will be quite strange and original. We conclude by noting the engaging nature of this task, impregnated with a strong sense of risk and creativity.

Firstly, we need to transcend our patriarchal urges to dominate and control. Life itself – largely unaided – can weave and knit those threads into something beautiful and constructive. And it is precisely at those chaotic and turbulent moments that we need to become highly imaginative in our minds and hearts, trandscending the rational, linear mind-set in preference for the creative, lateral approach. Our evolutionary vocation, as a human species, is to *co-create* and not to *dictate* what the creative process should be about.

Secondly, we need to transcend our inherited dualisms by opening our spirits to the inherent spiritual nature of all life. Our world is not a cold, inanimate object, driven by mechanistic, godless forces, but one that throbs with life and vitality. The very fabric of creation is not merely endowed with spiritual energy, but actually manifests – in a mysterious and tangible way – the divine creativity itself.

Finally, and perhaps most daunting of all, is the need to transcend our anthropocentric will-to-power, that addictive and manipulative human compulsion to perceive, judge and determine every outcome by the criteria of the human intellect as if it were the infallible mind of the Godhead itself. It is this idolatrous domination, whether expressed through the objectivity of the scientific method, the certainty of religious dogmatism, the competitive consumerism of market economic forces or the insatiable power of mainstream politics, that is driving the lethal forces of death and destruction all over Planet Earth today.

The major conversion needed in today's world is not the renunciation of those false gods that challenge mainstream religions, but rather the acquisition of the wisdom, honesty and courage to name the satanic forces we take so much for granted, forces that we ourselves have invented, and that we now exonerate and validate through assumptions and institutions that no longer stand the test of authenticity. The false gods of our time are not religious but primarily scientific, economic, political and ecclesiastical. The forces that threaten the future of our planet tend to be enemies within the gates of our perceptions and institutions rather than alien forces which threaten the existence of those realities we deeply cherish, but are, nonetheless, fundamentally flawed.

Reweaving a new tapestry of change is itself perceived to be threatening because it questions and undermines the comfortable world of what we know and cherish. But, in fact, it is largely a false world, and it is out of our very disillusionment with it that the urge to dream afresh and

159

construe anew ensues in the first place. At the end of the day, the will to meaning (and to new life) always prevails. It rarely impinges upon us in ways that *we* can manage. Yet it knows what it is about, driven by those subconscious forces – planetary and personal – that forever seek to make all things new.

Bibliography

Arbuckle, Gerard (1988), *Our of Chaos*. London: Chapman, and New York: Paulist.

Drucker, Peter (1989), *The New Realities*. Harper & Row.

Eisler, Riane (1987), *The Chalice and the Blade*. Harper & Row.

Gleick, James (1987), *Chaos: Making a New Science*. Heinemann.

Hamilton, Clive (1994), *The Mystic Economist*. Canberra: Willow Park Press.

Handy, Charles (1989), *The Age of Unreason*. Arrow Books.

(1994). *The Empty Raincoat*. Hutchinson.

Hawking, Stephen (1993), *Black Holes and Baby Universes*. Bantam Books.

McDonagh, Edna (1986), *Between Chaos and the New Creation*. Dublin: Gill & MacMillan.

Prigogine, Ilya & Stingers, Isabel (1984), *Order Out of Chaos*. Bantam Books.

Swimme, Brian & Berry, Thomas (1992), *The Universe Story*. Harper & Row.